Married to
a Legend
Don Pepe

To Muni and Marti
who made the last part of this journey with me.

José "Don Pepe" Figueres and Henrietta Boggs

Chapter I

I stood on the deck of the ship which was carrying me to a strange land, and watched the shoreline slowly grow more distinct. Waves swished languidly against a rocky promontory, protecting the wharf where banana boats were tied up before a string of warehouses. Overhead, huge billowy clouds pushed by the trade winds piled higher and higher against an azure sky. The driven clouds made me, too, feel as if I were being impelled towards a bewildering, new future for which I was unprepared.

Early the next morning the covered gangplank would be lowered to tunnel the passengers down onto "Costa Rica, the Land of Eternal Spring". So said the tourist pamphlets and picture postcards, and I believed every one of them. Growing up in Birmingham, Alabama, I had seen countless letters arriving for my mother with brilliantly colored foreign stamps; they were sent by her brothers in Brazil or Panama, with a steady stream coming from Costa Rica. I was twenty-one, the Second World War was in full blast, and I was bound for a visit to the Land of Eternal Spring to visit the aunt and uncle who had sent many of those letters with the exotic stamps.

As I watched the shore, banana leaves waved lazily in the gentle breeze. The night before, the ship had tied up in Bluefields, Nicaragua to take on a load of fruit. Since the weather was so hot the ship was loaded at night, and every seventy-pound stem of bananas was carried aboard on the backs of stevedores. Barefoot and stripped to the waist, they had bandannas tied around their heads to keep the sweat out of their faces as they struggled up the gangplank, bent over under the heavy weight. At ten foot intervals along their upward route, flaring torches swayed and flickered in the rising wind. The stevedores, their faces darkened by the sun and often pockmarked by disease or wounds, looked like a band of pirates preparing to pillage the small tropical port at the foot of the gangplank. And if the workers had looked up, there above the noise and heat and confusion, they could have observed the passengers standing on the afterdeck as the cooling winds rustled their starched white clothes. I gazed down and wondered what it would be like to carry bananas up a swaying gangplank in Bluefields, Nicaragua instead of travelling as a passenger on a ship in the United Fruit Company's Great White Fleet.

The next morning we disembarked. Standing at the bottom of the gangplank were my Aunt Ernestine and Uncle Vinell Long, two people I had met only briefly during my years in school. I remembered that he was witty and fun, and I would soon learn that she was difficult, heavy and dictatorial, given to lengthy sermonizing about everything. (Whenever she became particularly obnoxious, I comforted myself with the knowledge that thank God she was only an in-law and not blood kin.) Now, though, she was making an effort to be charming, taxing as it obviously was.

"I hope you'll be willing to accept life here on its own terms," she began, watching me with slightly bulging blue eyes which never seemed to blink. Though I sensed that she was trying to inject a modicum of warmth, there was still a slightly harsh timbre to the Kansas voice. "You'll have to be careful, though, about how you behave. It's different here."

"Perhaps you're exaggerating," Uncle Vinell said. "Foreigners have a little leeway."

Her face darkened, and I realized that she didn't like having her judgments questioned. "They don't have much. In fact, hardly anything. And you know perfectly well that we all have to be very careful."

Uncle Vinell turned away without answering. He picked up my two suitcases, matching grey bags with a red stripe around the top, and we started towards the railroad station. The luggage had been a birthday present when I was a sophomore at Birmingham-Southern College. I secretly felt that they were the first suitcases I had ever had which were worthy of me, a future world traveller who might not have been anywhere yet but who was destined to be a globetrotter crisscrossing limitless horizons.

As we made our way across the little town of Limón, my aunt spoke again. Her bulging eyes flicked over me and her voice held a tone of disapproval, which she would always use when speaking to me.

"I didn't know people your age still wore socks."

"College students still do."

I tried not to sound too defensive. Though she didn't say anything further, I couldn't help wondering why she disliked my clothes and disapproved of my socks. In this heat! It turned out that those first hours in Limón set the tone for my visit, and her attitude of condemnation was a constant presence during all the months I lived with her.

Limón was the main Atlantic exit through which much of the country's coffee and banana crops were shipped. In many ways the town was typical of most of the small Caribbean ports up and down Central America. Unpaved streets, raucous music pouring from innumerable bars, flies, dirt, naked children, loud laughter, and on top of it all the oppressive heat, so heavy with moisture you never seemed to feel clean. Aside from the postcard ocean views, the only thing I could call beautiful in the town was a magical park in the center of the square, its huge spreading trees offering shade and respite from the sun's bite.

As we traversed the park, my uncle suddenly pointed to a branch overhead.

"Look! Up there! It's a sloth!"

Motionless, seemingly not even breathing, he hung straight down from the limb, his four legs extended their full length, his black feet clinging to the branch.

7

"How long will he hang there?" I asked.

"All day. All night. He's so lazy it might take him an hour to move half a yard." My aunt's disapproval wafted upward.

We sauntered on through the town, the heat making us both drip unceasingly. Her face became redder and more moist as we moved along, not helped by the fact that Uncle Vinell seemed impervious to the temperature. His tall, slim body, flat as a board, turned out to have a thermostat fixed perpetually on normal, and was unaffected by ice, snow, heat, insects, hunger, fear or weariness.

"About half the population in Limón is black," he said. "Their forebears were slaves brought in from Jamaica to work the sugar plantations. They're prohibited by law from moving up into the highlands. Listen to the way they talk."

As we moved along I overheard their strange, sing-song kind of English, difficult to understand until the rhythm became familiar.

"Come, mon, you cahn stand me one glahss. I not much beer have to drink."

Across the street from us stood a low pink building with the words CANTINA BAR in green letters over the door. From a radio whose volume was turned up high, a roar of music reverberated down the street, banging against us as we stepped carefully through the garbage flung onto the sidewalk. We edged around an abandoned refrigerator, its blackened entrails spread at its feet as it sagged against a wall of the cantina. Four men who had looked upon the wine when it was red swayed helplessly with the bar's loose door which moved as they touched it. Groggily they swatted at the flies crawling over their stained and tattered clothes. They ignored a dog, every rib exposed, which slouched towards the entrance, only to be driven away again and again by the sluggish barmen.

This was the Land of Eternal Spring?

The narrow gauge train which was to take us up to the capital of San José waited in a small station. Steam rose from the miniature engine while the slender carriages, all their windows open, were already half filled. Barefoot vendors hawked trays of foods wrapped in dark green banana leaves, lifting them up to the passengers seated on wooden benches in the second class cars.

"What are they selling?" I asked. "What are those square things, like bundles, on those trays?"

"Those are tamales," Vinell answered. "They're made of ground corn filled with meat and vegetables, sometimes with raisins and olives. If they're well made, they're delicious." I was to learn later he had a voracious appetite and the digestive system of a boa constrictor, so his opinions about food were questionable. People hoisted themselves onto the train looking the way they did in most developing countries: bare feet, patched clothes, unwashed bodies and hair. With equal lack of concern they loaded and boarded chickens, stems of bananas, tattered suitcases held together with string knotted in a dozen places, bundles wrapped in sheets or quilts, and crying babies, all the while greeting each other with loud whoops of delight for everybody seemed to know everybody else.

"Juancito! Hombre! Como estás?"

"Todo va bien. Que tal la familia?"

"Bien. Solo la vieja anda afuera y me dejó solo con los chiquitos. Fijáte vos!"

The culture shock was stunning. This was my first trip outside the United States, the first time in a developing country, the first encounter with a society whose language I didn't understand. Since I was shy to being with, not speaking Spanish made me feel even more inadequate, and a sense of inferiority haunted me for months after my arrival. And though Latins were gracious and helpful with anyone struggling to learn their language, I couldn't escape the feeling that they were laughing at me for my inability to master Spanish. It turned out not to be true, of course; rather, they were making their own private jokes which had nothing to do with me.

"What are they saying?" I now asked, hating my inability to follow the conversations.

"Oh, they're just greeting each other, asking about the family, whose wife is visiting whom. Often they refer to their wives as la vieja, my old lady. But it's all full of fun."

We found our seats in the train and soon were lulled by the clackety-clack of metal wheels clanking over metal rails. Uncle Vinell had decided that during the eight-hour trip to San José he would teach me about the country and with only brief moments of respite, he kept me constantly informed.

"Well, within twenty miles we're going to start to climb until we reach an altitude of three thousand feet. It's pretty hot here, but San Jose is so cool at night you'll be sleeping under blankets. The plantations we're going through used to belong to the United Fruit Company, and were the most productive in the world. But not long ago they were all sold off to local producers; we'll have to see if the quality remains the same."

Every now and then there would be a break in the endless rows of banana trees and suddenly eight or ten houses would appear. As the train clanked forward I could see naked children playing in the dusty yard while in the doorways, thin, drooping women held babies in their arms.

"Is that where the workers live?" I asked.

"Yes."

"But that's terrible to make them live like that! Why can't they at least put screens in the windows?"

"When the Fruit Company built those houses they had screens. But the workers cut them out because they thought a screen kept out the breezes and made the house hotter."

"They must earn practically nothing."

"The Fruit Company always paid considerably above the local wage scale. But if the workers have too many children and the husbands drink too much, they'll always be like that. Anyway, as I say, since United Fruit sold out some time ago, it's no longer their problem."

Realizing that I didn't have any facts on which to base opinions, he tactfully changed the subject. "Many of these banana workers are Nicaraguans and have only a limited education. You have to be pretty tough to withstand the hard physical work, the heat and the insects."

The train clattered on. The flatlands blended into hills, green and blue against a glittering sky, and the air gradually became fresh and cool. Bananas now gave way to sugar. The prevailing winds pushed the slender cane leaves into green waves which rolled on endlessly across a section of hills, which reminded me of the backs of gigantic elephants. As we climbed higher I was surprised at how often we clattered over bridges, their long, spider-thin supports going down and down into bottomless valleys, the construction looking so fragile I kept wondering if the bridge would collapse before the train was half way across.

All along the route, my uncle kept up his barrage of information.

"Costa Rica only has about two million people, mostly descendants of Spanish or Italian immigrants. Many of them came in the Nineteenth Century, usually lawyers, teachers, and farmers, with hardly any soldiers among them. You'll notice later that there're no Indians, and except around Port Limón, almost everybody is white. Nearly all are small farmers. There're no huge estates as you have in other Latin American countries because everything here is on a small scale. And it's always a surprise to foreigners to find out how widely distributed the land is. That's also been the basis of its democracy."

The sun was sliding towards the horizon as the train labored ever upward. Across the sky my first tropical sunset began to flame and spread, scarlet and mauve with widening streaks of emerald green in colors I had never seen before.

In the tropics night comes swiftly, with no lingering twilight to foreshadow the stunning colors which will blaze along the edge of mountainous clouds before everything fades swiftly and suddenly turns black. Soon we would be reaching San Jose and the end of my eight-day journey by ship and rail.

Watching the breath-taking sunset, I told myself I would never go back, never return to Alabama and that suffocating Presbyterian world. I would never again be trapped in a routine of church three times on Sunday, church supper on Wednesday night, and the boring sermons endlessly repeating the same irrelevant themes. Never would I live in an environment where the black people were referred to as "those niggers," and where ninety-five percent of the population in many counties had never ventured outside the state.

Little by little the train began to lose speed. First up ahead, and then slowly all around us, the lights of a city started to glitter in the darkness. As we moved forward they spread out in every direction until we were surrounded by them. The train's whistle kept up a steady tooting as the passengers began to stand up and gather their belongings.

Aunt Ernestine turned to me. "You can carry the smaller packages. Vinell will take your suitcases. Put them there, Vinell," and she indicated a spot in the aisle near my seat. "No, not there. Over a little to the right."

The train gave an extra bang and a clatter, lurched once and then jerked to a stop. We had arrived.

I was so tired after the strain of travelling and meeting and absorbing that I have only a vague memory of reaching my relatives' house. I remember only that the large double doors opened after a rattling of keys and there stood the maid, dark and smiling. Her name was Carmen, a woman who had worked for my relatives for so long that she was now able to understand or guess at my aunt's impossible Spanish.

In a soft voice she began to speak, remarks which my uncle translated. "She's welcoming you to the house and hopes that you'll enjoy your stay."

I felt awkward and gauche. It was humiliating not to be able to make the automatic responses to her greeting which should have rolled unhesitatingly off my tongue. Instead, I stood there in a fog of embarrassment while she and Vinell carried on a steady chatter amid smiles and soft laughter. She kept observing me, making remarks which I was sure concerned me but which were, of course, incomprehensible.

"La Niña no es muy gorda pero se ve una persona simpática. Quantos años tendrá?"

"Más o menos veinte," my uncle responded.

"Se queda mucho tiempo?"

"Por lo menos varios meses."

Later I came to understand the Costa Rican custom of voicing personal remarks and observations about people right to their face. But now, not understanding increased my sense of disorientation, and I swore a mighty oath at that moment that I would learn to speak Spanish no matter what the cost.

"Did she say anything I should know about?"

"No, not especially, just that you're not very fat so maybe you should eat more. And that you're only going to stay a few months."

As we were turning into the house, Vinell added a postscript to Carmen's remarks.

"She also says you have a beautiful smile."

Mollified a little, I followed my relatives inside.

* * * * * * * * * *

The next morning I slept late—late by my aunt's standards, for to her eight o'clock was unforgivable. In the tropics and in agricultural societies, the day usually began at five with the first light. I soon learned it was a schedule my Prussian relative wanted her troops to follow. Her inflexible personality would not permit her to deviate one millimeter from the path she had chosen. Back straight as a ruler whether walking or sitting, eyes probing everywhere, one of the things she had decided on was to turn me into a sophisticated woman of the world who would reflect my aunt's values and lifestyle. Naturally, I resisted. Though none of this was ever openly discussed, and my realization of her plans dawned on me sometime later, I felt my objections grow stronger as the days passed. I wouldn't give in, and she wouldn't give up, so the struggle between us went on during all the months I stayed in her house.

After living with her for a short time I realized that Aunt Ernestine looked for three separate signs, before making a decision. The signs could be anything: a special verse from the Christian Science Book of Mary Baker Eddy, an invitation to a fancy reception at the Country Club, or an exotic plant someone had given her for an anniversary. If three incidents occurred in rapid succession that made her happy, she was convinced that her decision was the correct one—especially if that's what she wanted to do anyway. If, however, the decision brought unpleasant results, that meant she hadn't waited for the correct signs, and she had to punish herself for behaving badly. Sometimes she would contribute a hundred dollars to a cause she didn't believe in. For example, she would write a check to a liberal group who advocated policies she was opposed to, such as helping girls who were unmarried mothers, or paying for the confirmation fiesta of a Catholic friend's daughter in spite of abhorring Catholic dogma. No matter how often the signs failed her, she persisted to the end of her life with this habit, convinced that those signs were the only rational way to operate.

Breakfast on my first morning reflected the undeviating pattern of our lives, and characteristically, the meal never changed. Not once during my visit. As I was bathing I heard the clacking of Carmen's heels down the polished hall and then the banging of the front door. The scent of fresh coffee wafted through the house, followed quickly by my aunt's voice calling me to the table just as the front door opened. On each plate were fresh rolls still piping hot from the bakery. Then the indefatigable Carmen picked up two jugs, one with hot coffee, the other with hot milk. As she poured the light and dark streams simultaneously into my cup I could tell by their smell that I had never had real coffee before.

I asked for the blackberry jam made by Carmen from a recipe of Aunt Ernestine's. As Uncle Vinell passed it over, he continued my education of Costa Rica.

"Social customs in each society are so different. Here people feel it's more polite to reach across each other when they want something—even if they have to stand up to get it—rather than to interrupt by asking for the butter or jam."

"If I did that at home, reached across somebody like that, one of my brothers would probably have punched me, or at least yelled."

"Not here. People aren't aggressive in Costa Rica. There's very little violent crime. And almost no guns."

"Why is that?"

"They're just not given to harshness on a personal level. For example, you can't upbraid an employee even if he's done something wrong. If you raise your voice, he'll quit, then and there. This generally applies, though the banana workers have traditionally received very harsh treatment. But aside from that, on a national level, people here dislike the military so much that they tend to make fun of anybody in uniform. Since there's never been a military class in Costa Rica, people have developed ways of negotiating disputes. They just keep talking and talking and working towards a solution, and never feel they have to pick up a gun and kill each other. They especially won't get involved in a war."

15

During the years that followed I remembered that conversation about a society in which non-aggression was a way of life. It was as if destiny knew that I would have a need to understand. The memory was especially vivid the day I attended a ceremony, probably the only one of its kind in world history, when a head of state voluntarily disbanded his government's armed forces.

Chapter II

Four days after my arrival, my uncle and aunt talked about our trip to the farm, or finca, as we called it from then on, a word which all foreigners used even when speaking English. For years my relatives' unchanging schedule had been to leave on Monday afternoon, stay two weeks and return to San José to enjoy the delights of the city over the weekend. My coming had derailed their iron-clad plans, and my aunt was anxious to get the family back on track. I would have to accompany them on their trip because an unmarried woman of twenty-one could not be left alone in the city without a responsible adult or blood kin watching over her day and night.

Preparations for the trip led to much scurrying about, and this turned out to be the same for every trip. My aunt shouted commands from upstairs as Carmen's clacking footsteps raced to and fro. Uncle Vinell followed her instructions on slow, rubber-soled steps, while I stood around trying to help but only getting in the way. But my education prospered just the same. Uncle Vinell regularly pointed out objects all around me and taught me the Spanish words for them: the fresh, cooked, and canned comida went into special canastas and cajas; household supplies, including candelas and matches, found their way into alforjas (saddlebags). Larger tools, fertilizer, pruning shears, and the endless paraphernalia for three people on a remote farm all got themselves ready for travel. All the time we, the enlisted men, were aware that the Prussian guard monitored every smallest happening, her radar covering the entire horizon.

The afternoon was just beginning when the rented car and driver appeared, and we headed for the mountains. The driver was similar to many working-class Costa Ricans: not too tall, dark eyes and hair, skin tanned by the sun, and two gold teeth. Trying to be gracious, he made what sounded like a few friendly remarks.

"Buenas tardes," accompanied his soft smile."Que bonita la tarde."

Perhaps because she didn't understand, or because she felt that the driver was being too friendly, my aunt took instant exception to his meteorological observation, and began to huff and puff like a plump little engine building up a head of steam. After a few tentative bursts, she launched into a full scale harangue in her heavily accented Spanish, lighting up the horizon with flashes of anger, and then rumbling along with low-grade irritation at his innocent remark. After a few sentences the driver realized he was never going to understand the argument much less win it, so he scrunched down in his seat and concentrated on keeping the car out of the potholes in the road.

We worked our way over the hills which grew higher and higher, and finally turned into one of the blue-green mountains, Las Tres Marías, surrounding San Jose. As a Southern city slicker visiting a farm for the first time I had expected my uncle's property to look something like Scarlett O'Hara's plantation in Gone With the Wind. But when the car stopped in front of a rickety gate attached to a barbed wire fence which waggled in the wind, I realized I had not arrived at Tara. I had, in fact, arrived at La Hortensia, the name on the crooked wooden sign on the crooked, wooden gate of the finca. Meeting us there was the mandador, or foreman, Juan.

"Buenas tardes, Señores. Como están?"

"Buenas tardes, Juan. Que ha pasado aquí?"

"Nada especial. Todo va bien."

Unable to converse I smiled at him, received a silent greeting in return as he took the saddle bags and a lumpy sack I had picked up, and guided us down the path to the house.

It was a squat, ugly structure painted a mud-stained green. The roof was made of sheets of zinc now rusted to a tired brick color. There was one small window in each room, permanently nailed shut, and an open room at the back where large cement tubs for washing clothes took up all the available space. The porch across the front of the house was so narrow that one chair with one occupant constituted an impassable barrier.

Following the non-stop flow of instructions, I helped stash things away and then was shown my room. It was not exactly the throne room in Versaille Palace; barely large enough for a single bed and a table, it had no closet and no chest of drawers. Instead, there were five nails on one wall and a box under the table whose acid green paint had long since faded to a forlorn yellow.

"Just keep your clothes in there," my aunt said, indicating the box. "And when your boots get too muddy, leave them at the back door. And you can brush your teeth in the big tub where they wash clothes. And please remember to take a newspaper to the outhouse when you have to go to the bathroom. If you wrinkle it up in your hands, it does just fine." As she was going through the door, she called over her shoulder, "Oh, and before daylight is completely gone, get a candela and some matches. They're on a shelf in the kitchen."

It was nearly dark inside our small, four-room house. As I looked for the candles I noticed that a hall down the center cut our abode in equal parts: on the left the combined kitchen and living room where my aunt and uncle slept on two narrow cots, and on the right my room and a storage room behind. That was always kept locked because it held sacks of rice and black beans, tools, fertilizers and anything else my relatives thought a farm storage room should contain.

But as I fumbled my way down the hall, I couldn't understand why they insisted on living like this. No electric lights, no inside bathroom, no spacious corners in which to be comfortable during the six-months of rain when it was impossible to go outdoors. I could only guess that my aunt and uncle enjoyed pretending to be dirt farmers as a change from San José. They wanted to see if they could live off the land, eat black beans and rice like the peasants, and participate in the life of a working farm with no support system beyond what they themselves brought out from town.

The only concessions were the English language papers and magazines, which were always the first things to be packed. The Christian Science Monitor was included as was The National Geographic, TIME Magazine and an occasional edition of The New York Times. Although these journals were never forgotten and were among our dearest possessions, they created a certain tension. When one of us started to read an article and then left to go outside, hard feelings were expressed if we returned to find someone else had snapped it up. Uncle Vinell and I might sit wordlessly reading by candlelight or by the smoky lamp with its kerosene fumes and its wavering flame, but we made our irritation felt by rattling our pages in a sullen, threatening way. Needless to say, my aunt was impervious to such subtleties. Bolt upright, hair dragged back and fastened with large, black pins, she read until she was tired and then announced that it was time for the three of us to go to bed.

Before lighting my candle on this first night, I stood at the window and looked out at the darkening view with mountains all around, softly curved and dotted with clumps of trees. The moon came up as I watched. Twenty yards away beyond another barbed wire fence a slight declivity held row after row of low trees, their small white flowers glowing in the moonlight. As the light intensified they gleamed ever more brightly, like a vast carpet which seemed to undulate as the wind-blown leaves revealed their pale blossoms. Perfume filled the air. Rolling into my room on the waves of a breeze which kept sweeping around the house, the heavy scent seemed exotic and mysterious to my chaste Presbyterian nose.

I couldn't help wondering what changes that scent might bring? What wider horizons could a mere fragrance force me to follow?

The next day it was as strong as ever. "What's that wonderful perfume?" I asked over breakfast.

"That's a coffee field in bloom," Uncle Vinell answered.

"And there's nothing in the world more beautiful!" my aunt rhapsodized. "I've seen the tulip gardens in Holland and they can't compare. The coffee blossom will soon replace the purple orchid as Costa Rica's national flower. I'm sure of it."

During breakfast Uncle Vinell continued with my studies. "You were asking how coffee is picked. By hand, of course, berry by berry. Compared to most other work around the farm, however, picking is considered relatively easy work. The harvest season, which lasts for about three months, is a time of fun and games. It's the only period when men and women work side by side. Usually the men are off by themselves doing heavy work, and the women stay at home taking care of the house and looking after the children. But the picking season's different. Costa Ricans love to joke and have fun, and this is the time of year when they do it."

"It's also the time of year when the girls get into trouble," my aunt said ominously. "All that flirting—you can imagine what that leads to sooner or later."

Neither one bothered to tell me that the pickers were often tormented by flies and insects and that the basket they attached to their waist became heavier and heavier as the coffee berries were dropped into them. Or that the sun was hot and the hours were long. But even with their pay less than a dollar a day, they could live on it and feel comfortable with a job which provided extra bits of money.

* * * *

As the days passed I began to learn about coffee production. Like all agricultural processes it was slow and expensive, involving almost endless hand labor. A coffee tree takes nearly five years before it produces, and the first year's crop is rarely enough to cover costs. The seeds first have to sprout, then be transplanted into nursery beds, then transplanted again into their permanent row, then pruned, fertilized, weeded, harvested, dried on large patios, picked over and bagged. And all of these processes are done by hand—as they still are.

The finca stabled four horses. Like most Costa Rican riding horses they were small and gentle, with a slow pace and no great eagerness to take off and meet the horizon. I was assured that they were direct descendants of the Arab horses brought in by the Spaniards during the days of the Conquest. Since most of Costa Rica's wealth is based on land and agriculture, being able to ride was something you mastered as soon as you learned to walk. Furthermore, since country roads were unpaved except for a few two-lane highways, getting around on horseback was the most practical way to travel, especially for country people who couldn't afford a car.

Before the first week was over, Uncle Vinell had to go on horseback to do some coffee business at our nearest processing plant. Aunt Ernestine decided this would be a good time for me to learn to ride. A peon was dispatched to bring two horses for us, and one for the mandador. On the ride with Uncle Vinell, I could acquire some experience on staying upright on my steed.

"But I don't know how to ride," I wailed.

"Don't be silly," my aunt's inevitable response snapped back. "There's nothing to it. You just get on and ride, holding the reins like this—Vinell will show you—and always letting the horse know who's in control." I wouldn't have dared tell her that I didn't want to be in control. I just wanted the horse to like me.

We started out. Uncle Vinell wore his country uniform, faded khaki shirt and pants, a hat made colorless and shapeless by the weather, and high-topped leather shoes which at one time had had a bright polish but which now seemed perpetually covered with mud. He rode ahead down the curving, rutted road. I came next, and the mandador, Juan, last. (If we came to any gates that had to be opened, or a limb cleared away from the road, Juan moved forward to do whatever had to be done). And then we rode up the rutted road. And then down.

And then up. Blue-green mountains off in the distance, fat white clouds overhead, coffee farms in exquisite bloom, mile after mile—or kilometer after kilometer as the local people said, which seemed to go on forever.

"Is it much farther?" I asked after the first half hour, my fondillo feeling like a piece of hammered beef, numb now from the constant jostling.

"Oh, no. It's just a little farther."

With the restraint of a Christian martyr I refrained from asking how far a little farther was. We kept on. The sun got hotter, the road more rutted, and my feet jammed harder and harder into the stirrups as I tried to brace myself against the lurching of the horse. Occasionally we would pass a peasant family on the road. Most of the time the father walked ahead, carrying the larger toddler while the mother came behind, a baby in her arms, with the third and fourth children clinging to her skirt. Often there would be an older child, tall enough to shoulder a sack with the food every peasant family always carried.

The first travellers who passed smiled as the man took off his hat, and they all said "Dios", their voices soft and deferential.

"I thought Diós meant God," I called to Uncle Vinell's back.

"It does. But what they're really saying is adios, which of course means goodbye. But it's also used as a greeting. You'll notice people in San Jose say it to each other when they pass on the street."

"So you mean they say goodbye when they meet and goodbye when it's really goodbye?" I asked. Uncle Vinell let it drop.

I kept falling behind however hard I tried to keep abreast. The two men would slow down, pretend to be observing something in a coffee field or a drainage ditch and wait for me to catch up. And to keep my spirits from drooping too much, Uncle Vinell doused me with additional information.

"In another month, in May, the rains will begin. Here we have wet and dry, instead of hot and cold. If the temperature should ever go below 60, there'd be riots in the streets. And you'll see that it's never really hot either, at least not up on the plateau in San Jose where we live or here at the farm—and certainly never the way it does in Kansas where Ernestine is from, or in Alabama. Costa Rica is said to have the perfect climate."

We rode on. Every now and then we passed a peasant's house, its open door revealing a dim interior. There were usually two or three rooms in which half a dozen people lived and ate and slept and cooked amidst rattletrap furniture, a wood stove in one corner of the front room with the house often full of smoke, and a few chickens or maybe a pig rooting around the door. Usually there was a crucifix on the wall with which even Presbyterians were familiar—though we considered it papist and therefore suspect. But suddenly on the wall of a house we were passing was something I had never seen before.

As we rode by I asked, "What in the world is that—that—all bloody—thing on the wall?"

My uncle was baffled.

"That figure on the wall. Maybe it was Jesus, but it had a huge heart on the outside of its body. And it's holding its heart in its hand, with blood dripping down!"

"Oh," he said, "that's the Corazón de Jesús, the Heart of Jesus. It's just a statue and many Catholics have one like that. Probably Juan here does. They usually keep a candle burning before it. And they pray in front of it."

"But it's so bloody!"

"Different societies, different ways of expressing religion," was all he said, but I could tell that he disapproved of my provincialism.

24

As we rode on I was determined not to ask again how much farther because I knew he would give me the same answer. And I was beginning to have visions of being stuck on this beastly animal until I died of old age. The lower part of my body ached and I feared that when we did arrive I would be permanently adhered to the saddle. Just as I was about to resort to the stratagem of saying I had to go to the bathroom, (which would have embarrassed him because he was so Victorian), he suddenly spoke.

"There it is! The coffee beneficio where we're going. I have to talk to the owner, find out how much he pays for each fanega." I didn't ask what the two unfamiliar words meant, knowing that either he would explain them later, or that someone else would. All I cared about was getting off the horse.

I looked down into a valley stretched below me. Constructed along a small river was a collection of buildings and patios with a sign BENEFICIO SANTA ELENA. Since the processing of coffee requires lots of water, all beneficios in Costa Rica lie beside streams. Water flows into a series of skinny canals where the coffee is washed, stripped of its outer vegetable casing, washed some more, and then dried in the sun on large cement patios. And since the processing of coffee also requires lots of hand labor, I watched a brilliantly colored perpetual-motion show as everything along the valley floor appeared to be moving. Orange painted oxcarts dumped red berries into wooden shoots, men with wide paddles turned rows of golden coffee beans drying on white patio floors, other workers loaded coffee onto blue and red trucks lined up along a loading dock, peasants with bags over their shoulders went in and out of the store, and during it all, everybody talked or gestured or ate or in some cases, did everything at the same time. And pervading every nook and cranny was the scent of coffee, raw, wet, dry, or roasting for immediate consumption.

As we approached the main building constructed of white painted boards, the road spread out into a large plaza. At one end we found the office of the beneficio, and stopped when a man, obviously someone of importance, came forward to greet us. He was Don Antonio Figueres, one of the joint owners of the business, and the man who managed the coffee processing plant. As he talked his dark eyes twinkled as though he knew a secret joke which he would never tell because it would make everybody look so silly. After exchanging a few pleasantries with Vinell he gave us a bit of local color.

"You know, señor Long, the peasants around here call you 'don Mister Long.' They think Mister is your first name because your wife refers to you as Mr. Long when she's talking to them."

How can they understand anything she says, I wondered. Her Spanish is so awful they must think she's speaking English all the time. Though I was too shy to venture into any conversation with local people, even I could tell that my relative's accent was not quite up to Don Quijote's.

Uncle Vinell continued to chat with our host. "I hope your brother, Don Pepe, is well,"

"Yes, thank you. You are very kind. He is now in San José, but is planning to return this evening."

How formal they are, I thought,—and out here in the country, too. But maybe that's the way the Spanish are.

"Could we leave a message for Don Pepe? We're interested in doing some coffee business with your beneficio but we would prefer to discuss it in English. We would appreciate it if you would ask your brother to let us know when we could meet."

Taking an envelope out of his pocket, Vinell glanced at the note inside, then added a few words. He handed it to Don Antonio, we said goodbye, and turned into the small country store which all beneficios keep for the convenience of travellers and for their own workers.

"There is a song about owing one's soul to the company store. The peasants buy almost everything they need at these stores, and of course, are in hock for the rest of their lives. But it's the only place they have to shop without walking eight or ten hours to get to a village down the road."

In the store we bought some leathery bread and a luscious white cheese made in the area. I had seen enough of life on the farm to know that the milk from which the cheese had been made was not pasteurized, sterilized, or sanitized in any way. I further suspected I could contract hepatitis, but I didn't care. I was so hungry. And I also knew that as long as we were eating, we would not be on top of horses. Gulping down the cheese, I realized that if either of us became sick, I was going to be the patient. It was becoming obvious that Uncle Vinell's insides were made of copper tubing, that his whole life had been spent without a day in bed, and that he had not truly grasped the principle of the germ theory. As my mother's brother, the two were brought up to abhor illness and to believe that illness was somehow immoral. During their Victorian youth, they were taught to have faith in cold showers and the stiff upper lip. If a fatal disease attacked them, they would have the grace to die silently and not break any of the Crown Derby china as they toppled over.

While we were finishing our lunch and the slightly warm and loathesome limonada which was the only drink available Uncle Vinell referred to Don Antonio.

"He's very simpático, but it's the brother, Don Pepe, who is supposed to be quite unusual. Speaks English and I believe even studied in the States, Engineering at M. I. T."

"Was the note you brought— was that for Don Pepe?"

"Yes."

"What did you add?"

"Ernestine wants him to come to dinner. It'll be easier to discuss our business if we're in a home setting."

Chapter III

Across the hills there came the put-put-put of a small gasoline engine. Though we couldn't see the road we could follow the sound of the motor as it faded and swelled moving through the coffee fincas, dipping and curving and coming closer and closer. My aunt stood guard on the narrow porch waiting for Don Pepe. She had been up since daylight and had prepared, on our wood burning stove, a succulent lunch of roast pork, baked potatoes, vegetables and home-made bread. (This was the unvarying menu we always served whenever there were guests.) Since she had a degree in Home Economics from the University of Kansas, she was not only an excellent cook but enjoyed showing off her knowledge of nutrition and household management.

The sound of the little engine grew closer and louder. After three visits to the finca, I was becoming acquainted with the area and by now could more or less trace our guest's progress. In just a minute he would be at the gate leading into the property and then shortly at the fence separating our yard from the coffee grove I had smelled the afternoon I had arrived.

.Without looking at me Aunt Ernestine observed to the heavens, "I can't understand why you didn't bring something nice to wear, especially when we have guests."

"You didn't tell me anybody was coming," I protested, on the defensive as always.

"Well, hurry up and at least put on something clean. After that ride of yours, I'm sure you need to change."

Too late I turned towards my room, wanting to take off my uncomfortable riding boots and shed the old leather jacket which Uncle Vinell had lent me. But I couldn't escape for there was a sharp toot-toot of a horn, an engine being revved to keep it going, and a figure on a small motorcycle became visible through the trees. Then Uncle Vinell was opening the gate so that our visitor, José Figueres, known by everyone as "Don Pepe", could come in.

As I watched him park the motorcycle and walk towards the porch, I felt slightly disappointed. He did not meet my college girl standards. He was not tall or handsome or even attractive in the usual sense of the word. He had a strange little half-moon smile that was almost impish and olive skin tanned by the sun, and his English, though fluent, was accented and foreign-sounding. The only thing you noticed were his eyes, startlingly blue in that sunburned face, with black, black eyebrows going up into little peaks. Later I was to learn that his family came from a part of Spain, Catalonia, where his coloring, black curly hair and piercing blue eyes, were not exceptional, but now the combination seemed exotic and strange.

After an exchange of pleasantries, Uncle Vinell and our guest settled down to discuss coffee business.

"We will, of course, welcome your coffee crop," he said, "and we pay about the same as everyone else."

As far as I could tell, Don Pepe agreed to everything and seemed most anxious to have the privilege of processing the output of our farm. But after a while I got the impression that he was only half listening; though he continued to look at Uncle Vinell.

"And the young lady is your niece," he said suddenly, without any transition from the problems of coffee processing.

"Yes. She's from the South, from Alabama."

"I am only familiar with New York and Boston. I worked and went to school there. At M. I. T. But I am largely self-educated."

"That's much the best way," said Ernestine, in her Prussian manner. "People are too spoon-fed in school today. Over-indulged. I don't believe in that."

Don Pepe was quick to agree. "I grew up in a restrained household. No indulgence at all. My Catalonian parents would not permit us to put both butter and jelly on the same piece of bread. One or the other. Not both. Too extravagant. It wasn't the money; it was the principle."

"And in our home that principle was applied to everything," my aunt agreed. "We never wasted one single thing, never threw it away. Pieces of string, bits of thread, even Christmas paper from gifts was carefully folded and kept for the following year."

The conversation spun along, with Don Pepe and Ernestine agreeing about almost everything, a situation which did not exactly endear our guest to me. Perhaps, I reasoned, he was just being polite or maybe more than anything else, indifferent. But when the talk turned to politics, as it invariably did in this society, he became more intense. He sat forward in his chair, the electric blue eyes heating up so that they seemed to throw off splinters of light. Soon he launched into a condemnation of the government's corruption, where everything and everybody appeared to be for sale. And then he moved on to the extraordinary relationship between the Communist Party and the Catholic church.

"Have you ever heard of a stranger alliance? But perhaps it has a partial explanation in the figure of the Archbishop himself. He comes from a very poor family, and he feels deeply that something should be done to change the economic conditions here. Since he and Manuel Mora, the head of the Communist Party are friends, it may be that Mora has been able to convince him that the two organizations can cooperate to their mutual benefit."

At that moment my aunt abandoned her duties as a hostess, and standing so that our guest couldn't see, motioned me to follow her. In silence she hustled me along the path leading to the outhouse, her short, plump legs switching back and forth like oversized scissors. High above our heads, the huge scarlet flowers of my favorite tree, the Flame of the Forest, fluttered and swayed against a cloudless sky.

She leaned forward and lowered her voice. Almost from the first day I had met her, I had thought her a bit peculiar. Among other reasons she constantly fired off prophecies which I suspected never came true, though she was not at all inhibited by such details. With the certainty of an Old Testament prophet she would say, "Beginning the second week before Christmas a scorching drought is headed our way and the coffee crop will be ruined." Or, "I heard today at tea that Mrs. Richardson is starting an affair with Señor Fernández. I'm absolutely sure it's bound to end in suicide—a double one." Or, "The roof of the National Theater will come crashing down any minute, and it will be impossible to replace the antique crystal chandeliers." It was not the dead citizens that concerned her — they were apparently no great loss.

Now she pinioned me with her penetrating stare and announced her verdict.

"That man is going to be president! You must marry him! It's Fate! Fate! You were brought here for this purpose! There's not a doubt in my mind! Everyone has a purpose in life and this is yours!" Like Moses imposing the Ten Commandments, she issued a further order. "Now don't say no. Think about it! He's brilliant, he has large properties, and he comes from a good family. His father was a successful surgeon who had his own clinic."

"But I don't even know him! "

Her momentary silence indicated her contempt for trivialities.

"He has a magnificent future. I'm sure of it. I can tell by the shape of his head. It has the most beautiful curve there at the back I've ever seen!"

"But he's so old! He said he was thirty-four! I've never dated anyone who's already finished college in my whole life!"

My aunt's face took on a cement-like hardness. She had grown up on a farm in Kansas, the granddaughter of an immigrant German family who had fought drought, tornados, grasshoppers and bitter poverty, and she had no intention of letting her plans for me be derailed, once her mind was made up. Now she turned back towards the house. "We'll talk about it later. It's time for lunch."

"He's probably not even interested," I bleated. "He probably hates Americans."

Her blue dagger-eyes raked over my face. "Don't be ridiculous. You heard him say he's spent several years studying and working in the Northeast. He loves the United States. Otherwise, his English wouldn't be so fluent."

With this infallible reasoning we returned to the house. As we went in, I remarked to our guest that the motorcycle on which he had arrived looked like a practical way to get around over these unpaved, country roads.

He smiled proudly and announced one of his most important purchases.

"Oh, I've ordered a new one. A big Harley Davidson. The girl advertising it looks just like you. Here," and he began to grope through his pockets, "since I'm in love with this motorcycle—in Spanish it is called a motocicleta—I carry the ad around with me." He unfolded what turned out to be an almost life-size photograph of a beautiful girl, her long blond hair sweeping around her shoulders as she leaned languidly back against a huge, blue motorcycle. She was wearing a leather jacket and boots so highly polished the light splintered off the pointed toes.

Guileless as a child, Don Pepe stared at the picture. He seemed to regard the motorcycle as a kind of talisman, something with magic powers which would change his life and perhaps even influence his destiny. Mesmerized by the photograph, he gazed at the heavy machine, dazzled into a kind of silent delight. He hardly seemed to be breathing. Then reluctantly he dragged his attention from the photo and turned to me.

"The Americans make the best motorcycles in the world, much more powerful than the German ones.....I think you look like her."

I glanced down at Uncle Vinell's scruffy, discarded jacket missing two buttons in front and torn around the cuff and at the only boots I had which were now covered with hardened mud. It seemed impossible that even a man blinded by an obsession with motorbikes could believe that Blondie and I looked alike.

"The Harley Davidson arrives next week. I shall come and take you for a ride. We shall go to the volcano."

"Splendid!" my aunt boomed. "Come to lunch first. Just drop in any time. Our house in San José is in Aranjuez. Where do you live?"

"I have a small apartment not too far from you."

I learned later that Aunt Ernestine knew exactly where he lived and was already planning to send me on errands which would take me in front of his building. Then, if we happened to run into each other, she could be even more convinced that Fate wanted us to meet.

As he was leaving, we shook hands. "I still don't understand if the word 'don' is used with the first name or the last" I said to him. "Spanish is so hard for me."

"With the first. And I assume you know that mine is the most common one around, José. But everybody uses my nickname, Pepe."

The motocicleta burst into life. He waved as he turned toward the gate and the putt-putt of the engine gradually softened as he climbed the hill. After a moment, the noise died away. I watched my aunt, her gaze still lingering on the road up which Figueres, nicknamed Pepe, had disappeared. I turned to my uncle.

"Did you get everything settled about the coffee business?"

"Oh, yes, everything's all set. We'll send our coffee to him to be processed as soon as the crop comes in."

"That's nice, dear," responded my aunt, not listening. "His head is like a Greek sculpture. There's not a doubt in my mind he'll be president."

In due course, the blue Harley Davidson arrived and it was a spectacular chariot to behold. Everything on it which could shine, shone. And everything which could glitter, glittered. And the roar of its motor proclaimed that here was all the power and the glory which the internal combustion engine would ever need to conquer space and unpaved country roads.

We began to go out together. We would go to the Irazú Volcano and to inspect coffee farms and to visit his sister. As long as we were on the motorcycle, we didn't have to follow the local custom of being accompanied by a chaperone, and so we ranged far and wide. He showed me his country, with its exquisite blue mountains seemingly going on forever and the coffee plantations in fragrant bloom, with orchids growing wild in the mountains and bougainvilla vines flaunting their rainbow hues.

Gradually I learned to call him Pepe without feeling self-conscious. The daughter of a Presbyterian elder going out with someone named Pepe? Yes, and even becoming comfortable enough to correct the few mistakes he made in English. To my inexperienced and unsophisticated eyes, he seemed infinitely wise. He knew everything about his country with specific facts and figures; he knew everything about producing sisal which he grew on one of his fincas and then made into rope; he knew everything about philosophy which he could discuss in English, Catalán, Spanish, German and bad French. He also read Latin and Greek, had studied engineering and could recite poetry in three languages— which he did later with appropriate translations.

On the other hand, he couldn't do any of the things which I knew how to do. He couldn't dance or play tennis or make chocolate fudge or especially, flirt. In fact, I don't believe he had ever spent time with a girl. Women seemed to him a perplexing mystery, as baffling as they had been to Sigmund Freud with his wail of "What do women want?" I am not convinced that Pepe ever figured it out. He never seemed quite comfortable with any woman who demanded the right to be treated as an equal. In that one area he refused to budge; he would not outgrow his Nineteenth Century upbringing enough to free himself from his machismo. And it would be years before I would be able to untangle the mystery of why Pepe's relations with women would remain largely unsatisfactory.

But in those early days, the motorcycle seemed to appear more and more frequently at my door. He christened it Rocinante, after the horse ridden by Don Quijote, and it became our escape route, providing us with a chance to be alone and to get to know each other. There wasn't much of me to know. Since I had been a student all my life, and since he liked to talk, I got to know details of his life to a greater extent perhaps than he realized. Besides, if you're a passenger on the back seat of a motorcycle, you are the captive audience par excellence.

When we weren't on the motorcycle we would go out in his car. He had a beige-colored Dodge, large and comfortable, and almost always we would go with my aunt and uncle to have dinner or to ride through the lovely countryside or to brief business meetings when he had to discuss coffee production with an acquaintance.

There finally came the day when he invited my aunt and uncle and me out to his sisal farm, La Lucha. Since there were four of us, and since the rainy season had already started, we drove out in his car. We climbed up and up, crossed increasingly high mountains, slid down into valleys, worked our way over swaying bridges, eventually topped the final range and after coming around a bend in the road, he stopped the car.

In front of us was a wrought iron gate. Arranged in a slight arc across the metal bars of the gate were iron letters forming three Spanish words, Lucha Sin Fin.

"Step down, please. I want you to see the farm from here."

We looked down into a narrow valley, across a winding stream and on up to other mountains. Along the flanks and into the indentations, as far as the eye could see, marched row after row of sisal plants, their rigid, six foot leaves standing out from the main stem with military precision. Winding among the plants were narrow, rocky roads which struggled up the mountains, and as we watched, an oxcart loaded with fiber creaked and rattled on its way to the rope factory far below on the valley floor. Small groups of cottages painted bright blue and white and pink, the homes of the workers, wedged into niches of flat land hacked out of the side of the mountains. Hidden from our sight behind the curving roads were a soccer field, a school, a country store, an electric generating plant, an office, a machine shop and a large storage shed filled with rope ready to be shipped out to market.

"How long have you been working here?" I asked.

"Since I was twenty-two. I borrowed the money from my father and bought the property. None of this was here." He waved towards the plantations and roads below us. "There were only a few bits of rusty rope-making equipment and a leaky building. That's why I named the finca Lucha Sin Fin. Literally it means, fight without end or endless struggle. That's what life is all about."

I was consumed with admiration. The amount of human sweat and effort which had gone into the creation of this enormous enterprise took my breath away. How had he done it? In a spot this remote, without telephones, with hardly any roads and with everything having to be packed in by oxcart during six months of the rainy season, over impassible mountain trails—it was too difficult almost to imagine. Lucha Sin Fin, indeed!

Down in the valley a little later, in the center of the finca, we had lunch in his house. It was hardly better than a peasant's cottage, a flimsy wooden structure with a tin roof, its only distinguishing feature a collection of books spread over every table and chair and bench, and piled up in wobbly stacks in the corners of every room. On top of each column of books was a candela in a ten-cent candlestick, so that if the power went out, as it frequently did, he could continue reading by candlelight.

On an afternoon tour of the finca we came across a familiar sight. Just outside the machine shop stood the big, blue motorcycle being cleaned and oiled by a worshipful mechanic. As we walked passed, Pepe lightly patted the headlight, its polished chrome gleaming brightly in spite of the darkening sky. I remembered my observation the first day we had met when he showed me the picture of the motorcycle, and even then he projected a kind of spiritual kinship with his cherished Rocinante. Now, as we watched, his hand lingered around the headlight like someone touching a rabbit's foot, convinced it had special powers to bring him good fortune.

My aunt evidently thought so, too. Pulling me aside, she whispered loudly in order for him to hear.

"Can't you just see him when he's president, riding on that thing through the cheering crowds? They'll go crazy! And you right behind him!"

Chapter IV

Costa Rica in the 1940s, when I arrived as a college student, was a different world from the country it is today. Though its name means Rich Coast, (a misnomer if ever there was one) the country at that time was not only poor but for many of its people, almost hopeless. Half the population went barefoot. It was not uncommon to see young teenagers with teeth which were either completely rotted out or else largely false. Only the rare peasant stayed in school until the end of the sixth grade. Few country people had running water in their homes, much less electricity. Telephones outside the cities were almost non-existent, and those that were in place had been installed by private companies for their own internal use. The slums around most communities were pits of poverty and disease. To the majority of Costa Ricans, a checking account at a bank was something inconceivable.

The capital of Costa Rica is San José. When I arrived it had about 100,000 people. It was a sleepy little tropical city with purple bougainvillea climbing up every post and poinsettias growing ten feet tall and frequently used for fences. Spectacular blue mountains rose on every side, often with clouds brought by the trade winds artistically draped along their flanks. There was still a tiny electric trolley running down the main street, stores whose proprietors knew most of their customers by name, and a telephone system so inefficient that many offices kept little errand boys delivering messages around time because it was faster to send the child on foot than to try to get the operator's attention.

After two weeks on the coffee farm, my aunt and uncle and I returned to San José. In the post office box was a letter from Don Pepe.

Dear Mr. & Mrs. Long,

Thank you for your kind letter. For the next few days I shall be busy with work around the fincas, but in a week or two I would welcome the opportunity to discuss coffee business with you. When you have returned to La Hortensia, I will send a note with one of our trucks indicating which day I would prefer.

I appreciate your offer of hospitality and look forward to seeing you soon.

Sincerely yours,

José Figueres

That was the first time I saw the name which would one day become the country's most familiar name for the next fifty years.

With blinding originality Aunt Ernestine had christened our family The Three Musketeers, and we were as inseparable as our namesakes. I did not need as much togetherness as she did, but she had always wanted a daughter and when I turned up, she demanded that I fulfill that role. From the very beginning, however, I sensed that ours was not a relationship fashioned in heaven because I simply could not relate to someone who made me so uneasy. As soon as she entered a room, the atmosphere grew tense, and wondered what kind of a mood she was in.

As long as she was in the house I would try to prepare for one of her verbal attacks. During the early weeks of my visit, I was baffled by her outbursts because they seemed unprovoked and therefore inexplicable. Then I began to observe that her flares of anger were associated with not being included on the guest list of a certain party, or perhaps because she hadn't received an expected letter from her son who was managing a gold mine in Nicaragua. Or was the whole problem simply one of her obsessive need for control? And though I made certain never to be the cause of the outbursts, I received the blasts from her emotional cannons because I was often in the line of fire.

One day, not long after I had arrived, she asked me to help hang some curtains. They had just returned from the cleaners, and needed to have the hooks inserted at the top and then strung on the metal rod above the windows. But the fabric had shrunk and proved to be a foot too short. She was outraged.

"Look at that!" she stormed. "These stupid cleaners can never do anything right! I've explained to them a thousand times how to do it, but they're just too dumb to learn!"

Jerking the rod down, she clawed the hooks off, tearing some of the material in her rage. Then she wadded the curtains up into a heavy ball and slammed them down into my lap.

"Here! You deal with them!" She shoved a chair out of her path so hard it ricocheted against a table and then crashed on its side into a far corner.

My stomach went into a spasm of fear which kept jerking with the clack of her heels as she charged down the hall.

But of course I permitted none of my fears to show on the surface. I was too unsure of myself to discuss anything like that with her, or in fact, any other subject of a personal nature, and it's possible that she would have been shocked to discover that I was afraid of her. In any case, as a guest in her home, I felt that courtesy demanded that I yield to her wishes on almost all occasions.

Trying to deal with my fears I wondered if my attitude simply reflect too much passivity. Was my Southern dedication to courtesy a stand-in for cowardice? Perhaps, I reflected, I was doing nothing more than riding the surrounding waves, first of my aunt's conception of destiny, and then of Pepe's.

Would the time ever come when my own strength would reach such a level that I could generate surging breakers of my own?

* * * * * * * *

Now we began to participate in the social life of the city. To do so meant that I had to have clothes my aunt considered suitable, so we went on innumerable shopping expeditions. These always ended with my buying dresses which she liked but which I detested—or at best found only marginally acceptable. She favored colors which were muddy and drab. One skirt she insisted on buying was a sad, neurotic green to be worn with a particularly unnerving shade of palest mauve. From that we ricochetted to another level of sophistication, to trailing lace gowns or hats with dove grey plumes which made me equally uncomfortable. By my provincial, college-girl standards I thought I looked like a second-hand stand-in for Katherine Hepburn or worse still, someone's maiden aunt whose dress had been bought at the church bazaar.

A few hours before our first formal dinner, Aunt Ernestine began to explain how social life was carried on in San José.

"You'll find it different from what you're used to in the States," she said, that special harsh tone edging her voice.

"How?"

"Well, more formal. And girls have much less freedom."

"Even American girls?"

"Yes. Their reputations can be so easily ruined."

It sounded so ominous and so antiquated I wondered what happened to a girl when her reputation was ruined. Was she saved from falling on her sword by becoming a nun? Was she never again invited to the garden club?

"She has to be VERY careful."

As Ernestine talked she marched up and down, her short, stumpy legs like pistons driving her around the room. Since she was only a little over five feet two, she always wore high heels, even in the house performing her household overseer's role. The sound of her heels clacking on the uncarpeted floors indicated her state of mind. If the clacking were rapid, she was agitated; if it slowed down, she was in a rare mood of relaxation. Now she ended her discussion by making another of her prophesies.

"You'll see tonight how everyone behaves. If there're any young men there, you can be sure there'll be complications!"

The formal dinner took place at the home of a member of the British colony. George Lyon had come out from England towards the end of the Belle Epoque. Not facing much competition, he made money in banking, sent home for his childhood sweetheart, built a big house at the end of the Avenida Colón, and settled down to raise a family. The house, set in an English-style garden, was a strange mixture of Merrie Olde England and colonial América Latina. A wide verandah shaded by stately palms interspersed with coffee and orange trees encircled the home. On the tables in the drawing room were copies of The Tatler and The Illustrated London News. A grand piano in one corner had books of music scattered around, with The Merry Widow Waltz open on the rack. Brilliantly colored tropical plants in big tubs were everywhere, adding a foreign note to this most English of rooms.

But it wasn't the flora so much that caught my attention as it was the family photographs. Dozens of them, all in silver frames, some picturing ladies in the hour-glass gowns and feathered hats of the 1890s, others showing mustachioed gents in regimental uniforms guarding the Khyber Pass. There was one of a hunter in East Africa," old Uncle Nigel, you know, dear," with a foot on the back of a slain lion, and assorted nephews in the uniform of the RAF, climbing into or out of their fighter planes, for the Second World War was in full swing. On one wall was a life size photograph of King George and Queen Mary, stately and formal, he rigid with medals and a sword, she solemn amidst lace, ropes of pearls, and a diamond tiara. For a fleeting moment after every meal this couple moved front stage center among their guests to receive our tribute in two muted words.

Needless to say, I was enchanted. It was all so worldly, so continental I could feel Alabama dropping away by the cupful. Of course, we had dressed for dinner, because at the Lyons' home it was always black tie. The family even dressed when they were alone. Out in the colonies one had to keep up one's standards or one might start slipping and finally go native. Perhaps that was why delicate cucumber sandwiches were still served for tea every afternoon at four, and why there were Jamaican servants who spoke English rather than local maids who only spoke Spanish.

On this evening, the guests sipped drinks for half an hour and then at exactly 7:45 one of the maids appeared in the doorway of the drawing room. She wore a scarlet turban which soared above her dark face, and a striped dress down to the floor. Impersonal as a statue she stared over our heads and majestically delivered her message.

It was at the dinner with the Lyons that I first heard the name of the communist leader, Manuel Mora. The conversation about the worsening political situation wound on. Two of the guests were representatives of large American corporations, another had his own company, and all were relatively well-to-do. None of them saw any reason to change the way society was organized. But they all agreed that President Calderón Guardia was a disaster.

"I'm afraid that corruption is on the increase," said Alex Murray, head of a large coffee firm. "My manager went to get a permit last week, to import some machinery, and the man in the Interior Ministry demanded to be paid off. That wouldn't have happened before."

Later, Uncle Vinell, my walking encyclopedia, supplied a few details about Mora. "He's the leader of the Communist Party here, and he's sincerely convinced that the capitalist system has failed. He says it took the Second World War to pull the world out of the unemployment caused by the 1929 Depression. So he feels we should try something else. And after spending some time in the Soviet Union, he believes that the communists have the answer."

Uncle Vinell's detachment about almost everything often surprised me. In spite of his deep conservatism regarding politics and economics—after all, he was a banker with the attitudes of a proper Victorian—he could still discuss Mora with a calmness few people at that time could equal. Uncle Vinell was convinced that Mora was wrong in his conclusions, but there was no suggestion that he should be exiled or even forced to keep quiet. Rather, as long as we were all talking to each other, perhaps the communists could be persuaded to change their mind.

Following my aunt's admonition to observe the other young women's behavior, I kept an unblinking eye on the three fellow guests who fell into the right age and sex category. But there was nothing about any of them which seemed unusual. Aside from their long, black gowns they looked like my fellow college students back in Alabama. A little later, after I grew somewhat more accustomed to my aunt's patterns of behavior, I realized that her dire warnings of disaster rarely came to pass and should properly be ignored.

As soon as dinner was finished, the ladies withdrew to leave the men alone with their cigars and cognac. But just before the hostess shepherded the delicate sex upstairs to have our coffee and to repair our makeup, we engaged in a final ritual repeated all over the British Empire. All the guests stood up and turned to face the large photograph on the wall in its heavy, gold-embossed frame. Moved by a signal which escaped me, we raised our glasses and in one voice solemnly said, "The King".

* * * * * * * *

As the weeks passed and we went out whenever we were in town, I realized that I knew nothing about society in a small town. I had grown up in Birmingham, Alabama, a relatively large city, and I found it hard to adjust to a country where the guiding light in any social situation was concern over what the neighbors would say. I learned very quickly that they would always say a great deal. And to everybody they met. Or could reach on the phone. "Society", at that time was composed of a small group of the Costa Rican elite, all of whom were either related by blood or marriage, or else who knew each other by name—plus the American and British colony. It was this latter group that I belonged to because my aunt and uncle considered themselves mainstays of the colony.

For years in both Central and South America Uncle Vinell had been head of different branches of the Royal Bank of Canada. As Mr. Moneybags, he had enjoyed considerable clout both socially and financially. Typecast for the role of a Victorian banker, he wore conservative, three-piece suits, gold cuff links and a pocket watch with a gold chain across his flat stomach. By the time I arrived his dark hair and precisely trimmed moustache were already streaked with grey. On all occasions his trousers were pressed to a knife-like crease above black silk socks and black shoes gleaming with recent polish. Through round, wire-rimmed glasses he regarded the world with a kind of humorous skepticism, prepared to accept the frailties and deceptiveness of his fellow citizens as part of the human condition. A year or two before my arrival he had retired from the bank and had bought the slightly run-down coffee farm where we had just spent the preceding

46

two weeks. Nonetheless, he was still treated with elaborate courtesy because it was assumed that he still had considerable influence with the bank's managers and therefore would have a say about who would be allowed to borrow money.

Whatever their varied backgrounds, the Anglo-Saxon groups had one thing in common. They knew they were superior. Not because of wealth or culture or knowledge. Not because they spoke fluent Spanish for most of them, no matter how many years they had lived in Latin America, could hardly say good morning. In fact, their attitude about language was that people needed to learn to speak English. No, the Gringos didn't have to explain or to justify; they were just superior. They had blue eyes and light skins, and they spoke English as a mother tongue. They also came from countries which supplied the financing for the local products and the markets where those products were sold, as well as the technology and the military might for much of the rest of the world. And besides, as everybody knew, it was only the superior who could bear up under the weight of the White Man's Burden.

While many of the other Gringos did not live on the same baronial scale as the Lyon family, a large income was not required in order to spread oneself a little. Maids were cheap and ruthlessly exploited. In the main, they were girls coming into town from rural areas, and they considered working ten hours a day inside a house better than their alternative, which was picking coffee in the fields. Since there was no legislation protecting them, they were paid as little as their employer could get away with. Besides, many of these girls were single parents. Birth control was prohibited by the Catholic church, and the young women of the country had neither sexual knowledge nor any means of contraception. After a one-night, brief encounter, quite often the woman became pregnant and, in the classic scenario, the man disappeared. Therefore, she considered herself lucky to have someone else's roof over her head and her child's—no matter how little the pay.

Not long after my appearance in Costa Rica, I was taken by my uncle to the club to play tennis. He wore white linen and was somewhat disconcerted when I appeared in red striped shorts and a red shirt. It was only later I learned that the gentry were expected to stick to whites, all of which had to be hand washed by the maids because washing machines were largely unknown. That day was also my first encounter with a ball boy. Ten years old, barefooted, hungry-looking, he waited several feet behind me back of the base line. I didn't understand why he was there but was too embarrassed to ask. At the first missed ball, though, everything became clear. When I started after it, my uncle's voice stopped me.

"Let him pick them up. That's what he's for." I stopped though it somehow seemed self-defeating. If the purpose of the game were exercise, having someone else do part of it for you took a smidgen of the bloom off the peach. But it turned out that was also part of the White Man's Burden—in addition to ignoring the boy, we were brought chilled orange juice after the sun got too hot and drunk it in front of him although he desperately needed it more that we did.

For women in a colonial society, life could be both physically and mentally deadening. In countries where servants are cheap, the weather benign, and women are tethered to the house by social custom they had little to challenge their minds or even to fill up their days. So that an inordinate amount of time was spent looking for things to do. One of the things we did was to "See People Off."

One morning at breakfast my aunt informed me of our day's activities.

"Mrs. Harrington is leaving for England, so we're going down to the station to see her off." Then she turned to me. "Wear your black and white silk. And that little hat with the veil. And don't forget your white gloves."

I stared at her, almost too surprised to speak. To dress like that at ten o'clock in the morning just to go to the train station! But to the end of her life Aunt Ernestine remained in the grip of her Prussian upbringing, inflexible and humorless, and I knew that when she announced white gloves were de rigeur my

48

objections were useless. She knew exactly how life was supposed to be conducted, and she dedicated herself to seeing it carried out.

Promptly at ten o'clock we presented ourselves at the station, appropriately dressed. To an American used to the idea that bigger is better, the train station looked like a miniature Victorian building for children to play with. It had metal gingerbread trim at the edge of the roof and a brown and white tile floor and about six or seven wooden benches accommodating three people each who patiently sat inside the station staring up at the grilled ticket window. And the train itself was a perfect match. A narrow-gauge string of cars, slender and delicate, waited at the platform for the passengers, while the baby engine spewed out smoke just to let everybody know it meant business. It was the same train that carried me from Limón to San José the day after I had arrived in Costa Rica.

Then it was time to go. Mrs. Harrington, majestic in a navy blue print with matching coat and hat, shook hands all around, clutched her parasol and large, bulging purse, and turned towards the steps of the train. They were so narrow and she so rotund I wondered for a moment if she would be able to squeeze aboard. She addressed the group in general.

"Do keep an eye on my delphiniums," she implored, her voice flute-like and slightly quavering. "And the roses have to be dusted every week. And check on Alfonso. He's taking care of the cat." She, of course, mispronounced his name, but since she had been doing that from the first day of his employment, no one even noticed—All the other foreigners mispronounced the native's names. Then Mrs. Harrington hoisted herself aboard the velvet curtained car, we all waved as we promised to write, and the slow clack-clack of the wheels gently bore her away.

We turned towards our cars, trying to avoid the beggars who touched our sleeves, silently demanding conscience money because we were rich and they weren't. They mingled with the small boys who kept trying to sell us three or four loose cigarettes which were slightly dirty, and packs of chewing gum which had sometimes been opened.

Almost everybody in those days travelled by sea. They would leave San José by train, go to the Atlantic Coast to get a ship, and then relax in the knowledge that they would be spending a week or ten days on board. And it was the same coming back. Therefore, most trips to be worthwhile would often last two or three months and required a prolonged separation from one's friends or family.

On one occasion we saw some people off on a Sunday, so my aunt and uncle decided that after the train left, they would take me to see the Military Mass. Though my relatives were not Catholics, they were determined that I should participate to as great an extent as possible in the life of the country, and the Military Mass was a sight to behold. A platoon of soldiers, lead by a drum and bugle corps, marched up the steps of the cathedral and down the central nave to within a few feet of the altar. The officer at the head turned smartly to face the flock, and snapped out a command.

"Atención!"

The soldiers did one or two fancy movements with their guns as they tried to look military, but their wrinkled uniforms and slightly ragged lines didn't look particularly convincing.

"Presenten armas!" shouted the officer. And the rifle butts crashed down on the tile floor with a deafening clatter of metal and wood and then snapped up onto every rigid shoulder. As the soldiers presented arms to God, the drum let out a smart military roll and the bugles burst forth into a shrill paean of praise.

The effect was stunning. Within the silent cathedral the clatter of arms and the military music jolted us all, made more shocking by our surroundings of incense, stained glass windows, and the Virgen Mary holding up the Prince of Peace. The congregation loved the Military Mass because they didn't have to kneel down or stand up during the proceedings, and especially because they didn't have to listen to the priest telling them to stop committing all those delicious sins or they would burn in hell.

And then, as suddenly as it had begun, the music ended. The officer stomped around to the head of his troops, his shouted commands rang out again, and the heavy, military boots crunched the floor as the column rattled its way along the nave and out into the open air. As soon as the cathedral was silent again, the officiating priest mounted the pulpit and raised his hand to make the sign of the cross over our bowed heads and to bless us in the name of El Padre, El Hijo y El Espíritu Santo.

As we came out into the street, Uncle Vinell said, "That's what the Costa Ricans like to use their military forces for, presenting arms to God."

We began to stroll down the Avenida Central, the main street of the city when Uncle Vinell made a comment that surprised me. "Do you know enough about history to know that every society on every side in every war always invokes God's help in fighting its battles? He must have a difficult time sorting out all the demands for assistance." And then, disconcerted or expressing such a Victorian thought, he lapsed back into silence and never mentioned the subject again.

In those days, San José was such a small town that the gentry knew everyone who was anyone, most of whom we saw every day when we went "into town." As a matter of fact, that was one of the reasons we went into town, to see everyone we knew. If any of the gentry had unmarried daughters, the girls were guarded as though they were commodities to be sold—and to a certain extent, they were. If they married, and especially if they married well, they were then cared for till they died and the family derived numerous peripheral benefits. But if they didn't find a husband, they remained a burden on their parents and after that, on their siblings, until the time of their death.

The one thing demanded by men in choosing a wife was not brains or ability or charm or even wealth. It was virginity. She had to be pure. And families saw to

51

it that she remained untouched. Girls were not permitted to be alone with men until an engagement was announced—which often took place when the young woman was only sixteen. Until that moment, daughters were always accompanied by someone from either her family or his, and it didn't matter who it was. There just had to be someone nearby who was still breathing and who presumably could see well enough to be able to report to Mamá or Papá if any hanky panky had gone on.

It would be only a few short weeks after my arrival when I would begin to experience the unblinking eye of Big Brother—in the form of little nephew.

Chapter V

We moved back and forth between the finca and the city, and life in town convinced me that I was not born to be the handmaiden of growing things growing. I felt then and still feel now that once you've seen spectacular scene, it is sufficient. There is no need to linger. The mind needs constant stimulation, and as a city slicker born and bred, I could only find satisfaction in the city.

We had returned to town not long before Christmas. My relatives had announced that we wouldn't exchange gifts, wouldn't put up a tree, and wouldn't decorate the house. Their only son was not coming home for the holidays so Ernestine and Vinell had decided to try to ignore the season and pretend it didn't exist.

I felt a pang of regret at my aunt's announcement for this was the first time I had ever spent a Christmas either away from home or in an environment which did not participate in the Yuletide madness.

Not far from the center of San José is the Church of the Good Shepherd. It is an Episcopal church, sitting back from the busy street, its old stones now softened by time and weather to a pale, ecclesiastical buff. During my years in San José, it served the British and American colony as a place for weddings, christenings, and burials. Though the weekly congregation was not large, on important holidays like Christmas and Easter the church would be packed with people who were described as "the poinsettia and lily crowd."

On my first Christmas away from home I was dying of homesickness. I was used to a houseful of brothers, sisters, and cousins, a tree bowed down with scruffy, handmade decorations, and packages being wrapped in hidden places and then sneaked under the tree to the surprise of everyone.

Early on Christmas Eve I went alone to the church, hoping at least to hear some familiar carols to help assuage my loneliness. But I was not so lucky. Instead of the old favorites I longed for, "Silent Night" and "Oh, Come All Ye Faithful", the hymns had been chosen by an English clergyman for a service I was completely unfamiliar with. Is there any loneliness more intense than a young person's first Christmas away from home, with no one there to fill up the empty places or no one to set the framework for the beloved rituals? In fact, it was years before I could deal with Christmas without a catch in my throat and a desire to cry all the time.

Miserable and lonely, I arrived back at the house. Since the garden gate was always locked we gained entrance by rattling and banging the iron chain fastening the gate to its supporting posts. I rattled and banged and then called out the Spanish word I'd been taught.

"Upe!" It meant something like 'anybody home?'

Carmen came out with the key, and I followed her along a wide cement path through the front lawn, across a porch running the width of the house, and thus to the tall double doors leading into the entrance hall of our big two-story, wooden structure. (Needless to say, as a young, unmarried woman, I was not given a key of my own; that would have implied too much independence and friends and neighbors would have thought I had too much license.)

Carmen, her dark eyes snapping with intelligence, now preceded me across the porch, chattering without a break. My Spanish had reached a point where I could understand a great deal, but could hardly say anything. And what I did understand was often not what the other person was saying.

"Estamos preparando una fiesta. Es una sorpresa, con frijoles y arroz y carne y frutas. Muy bonita la casa, con flores y candelas. Muy elegante todo!"

I wasn't sure about anything except that somewhere there was a fiesta. But as the doors swung open, I could hear my aunt's clicking footsteps trotting from the kitchen to the dining room and her voice issuing instructions to Uncle Vinell.

"Now, fold the napkins to show a three inch border. It has to match the lace tablecloth. And be sure to light the candles on the sideboard, the ones in the tall silver candlesticks. They'll help show off the bouquet in the center of the—"

Her voice stopped as Carmen and I reached the door of the dining room. For a second I thought the place was on fire because there were flames everywhere, from candles in clusters and alone, reflected in the mirror over the sideboard, gleaming from silver and polished wood, refracted from crystal goblets set about the table. Resplendent in black satin and long strings of pearls, Aunt Ernestine for once stood silent and still, watching me with eyes that seemed suddenly softened by the candlelight. Then she spoke and even her voice had lost its harsh undertone.

"We thought we'd have a surprise Christmas Eve feast. You seemed a little homesick. I remember the first Christmas I spent away from home. It was awful."

Oh, God, I thought, I'm going to start crying! And I promptly did, the tears sliding down my cheeks as I tried to wipe them away. Of course, I had no handkerchief so all I could do was stand frozen with embarrassment, my head down as the tears dripped through my fingers. From far away my aunt's voice reached me, now returning to its usual tone of command.

"Oh, for heaven's sake, don't be such a baby! Go and wash your face. And put on a clean dress. Don Pepe is coming for dinner."

As I turned on the lights in my room I saw on the bed several packages wrapped in Christmas paper. In spite of our agreement about no gifts, my aunt had provided me with a bundle of presents, including the first silk underwear I had ever owned—in fact, ever seen. Exquisitely embroidered, the fragile wisps of silk slid through my fingers, paper thin and almost transparent, lace along the edges, spaghetti fine straps and a wicked slit up the side of the slip.

A noise at the door made me turn. Ernestine stood there observing my reactions. On an impulse I kissed her, the first spontaneous gesture of affection she had ever awakened in me, and mumbled my thanks for her gifts. Taken a little aback, she pushed me away.

"Hurry up. He'll be here any minute. Put on your pink silk. It's good with your skin."

In honor of our guest, we had a traditional Costa Rican Christmas Eve dinner, paella, tamales, black beans, and tortillas, with several side dishes, as well as salad and fruits and cake. Instead of the Christmas Day feast of northern countries, in most of Latin America the holiday meal was served at midnight on December 24th, and in a family with children, that was the time when gifts were distributed and toasts drunk to the season. But my relatives found it was too long to wait until the witching hour so Don Pepe had been invited for about nine thirty.

Our guest arrived at exactly the appointed time, bringing gifts for us all, even the maids. From a large bag he began to take out the packages which he presented to each of us in turn with an awkward little bow. The first gift went to Aunt Ernestine.

"This is for you," he said, handing her a large, lumpy bundle. "You said you liked exotic plants. See if this is exotic enough."

He watched while she carefully undid the package without tearing the paper, and I knew that next year that same wrapper would enfold another gift.

"Oh, you shouldn't have! I've never seen anything more unusual!"

The next bag yielded a bottle of wine which he presented to Uncle Vinell.

"This is a special Spanish wine from Catalonia given to my father by a grateful patient. I am aware that you do not drink very-"

56

"None at all," my uncle interrupted. "We're Christian Scientists and our religion forbids it."

"I see. But since nothing must be wasted, perhaps you could offer it to friends when they come to dinner."

Then he turned to me. "On one occasion you mentioned that you liked poetry, so ..." and he handed me a book.

"Oh, that was—" I stopped, not knowing how to phrase it. My inclination was to say, hey, that's wild, but I suspected that he would have corrected me. Instead, I opened the book and my heart sank. Oh, God, ninety-seven pages of Spanish poetry! I'll never be able to understand a word!

Perhaps he saw the consternation in my face because he seemed to feel compelled to offer help. "I will be pleased to translate it for you if there are parts you do not understand. There are times when poetry can be difficult—though it says so much more than prose."

"I'd like to try first myself, but I'm sure I'll need help. And thank you for the present."

With unwonted tact I refrained from pointing out that he need not feel it necessary to go through the whole book at one sitting—something I was sure his driving personality would have compelled him to do. And I suspected he was not capable of understanding that too much poetry, like too many funny stories at the same time, could bring about a nervous tick in the listener.

Since I hadn't known he was coming I did not have a gift for him. Ordinarily, that would have embarrassed me, but my uncle saved the day. From a heavy carved table he picked up a package wrapped in more used paper which, from its creases, I judged to be at least three Christmases old.

"Ernestine and I would like you to have this."

Pleased as a child, Don Pepe squeezed the parcel with his swift, economical gestures, and then smiled.

"I hope it is a book."

The same careful unwrapping followed, and then he opened the book, an antique, leather-bound volume, his smile stretching wider and wider as he slowly leafed through the pages.

"You could not have given me a present I would have valued more. Abraham Lincoln is a man I have admired since I was a child. This copy of his speeches I will always cherish." Another page was turned. "Of course, I know 'Four score and seven years ago' but there are many here which will be new to me. What a brilliant man he was! I am convinced he knew more about the vagaries of the human heart than most political leaders."

Still holding the book, he launched into a description of his life in Boston and New York. He had held two jobs while he studied English and Engineering, had enjoyed as much of the cultural life of the cities as he could afford and had returned his father's monthly checks sent to cover his expenses; he had insisted on supporting himself without any help from home. Then he stopped suddenly in the midst of a sentence.

"Do you remember the scene in Othello where he is telling Desdemona about his battles against the Turks?"

I nodded, wondering where the conversation was going. Surely, surely, he wasn't planning to make a comparison between those bloody battles on land and sea, and the problems of finding a job in Boston. But he did. And he meant every word. Years later I remembered that conversation. When I once discussed the characteristics which go to make up a great leader, I realized that a sense of humor is not one of them. He cannot afford it. The conquest of power is so difficult, and controlling events requires such total dedication that the detachment necessary for humor cannot be indulged. It is a luxury too costly for the leader even to consider. And Don Pepe, for all his enormous contributions to his country and to Latin America, could never be accused of the light touch.

After that evening we went out more and more frequently. Almost always my aunt and uncle went with us, either invited by Pepe or at a suggestion from them. Sometimes we went to strange restaurants which were not very good but which, in my naiveté, had what I considered a certain atmosphere. Or we went to the Union Club, the fanciest place in the city, which Pepe disliked because he felt ill at ease. It wasn't until years later that he could enjoy himself in elegant surroundings, for he could never relax except among people who were of modest circumstances. What he did enjoy most of all, were people with a special expertise whom he could question.

One afternoon when my relatives were busy, Pepe arrived in his car. He had invited me to go to a beneficio owned by some wealthy Germans who had imported a new type of mill for drying coffee. As I came out to the car I saw sitting in the back seat a small, brunette child, his black eyes and hair nearly hidden in the dark upholstery. Pepe's introduction was casual.

"This is Román, my sister's son."

The boy smiled shyly but didn't speak. Then he settled back in his corner and stared out of the window. But when we went to the beneficio, when we went to have coffee, when we went to the post office for stamps and letters, Román was there, three or four steps behind like a silent, dark shadow, unobtrusive but ever present.

No explanation for his company was ever volunteered. After the third or fourth time, though, I began to wonder if he were a problem child who could never be left alone at home. Or if he and his older brother harbored a secret hatred or a family feud, and that the two had to be separated to avoid a fratricidal crime.

Finally one day I asked my aunt for an explanation.

"What's going on? He's the best behaved child I've ever seen but he's just always there. Why do you suppose Pepe insists on bringing him?"

"Well," she began, "he probably wants —"

But this time it was Uncle Vinell who interrupted.

"The little boy is your chaperone."

"But he can't be more than eight or nine years old," I protested.

"Just the same, that's what he is. And as long as people can see that he's always around, they'll know everything is as it should be." Needless to say, my Victorian relative could never do more than delicately imply that even the thought of impropriety was out of the question. In his eyes whether Román had been there or not, nothing—ahem!—untoward would have happened.

But a thought suddenly occurred to me. "Maybe he's not just protecting my reputation. If Pepe's so concerned about our never being seen alone together, maybe he's protecting himself just as much. He doesn't want people saying that he's the kind of man who would go around with a —"

I stopped, trying to conjure up a word sufficiently derogatory to describe a woman who, in the Twentieth Century, would dare go out alone and unchaperoned with a man who wasn't a close relative.

But before anything black enough came to mind, Vinell broke in. "You may be right. That hadn't occurred to me but if Don Pepe is so adamant, yours may be a correct guess. Why don't you ask him?"

I thought about how to phrase my inquiry. I was too unsure of myself just to blurt out the question, and he was not the kind of man you demanded personal information from. There was a reserve about him, a certain distance he preserved in his behavior which kept people from coming too close. It was not a matter of language or cultural differences. He just never let his guard down, never let anyone feel that he would spontaneously reveal anything except the bits and pieces of himself he was willing to allow observers see.

Most of this I intuited rather than knew. But when I finally got around to asking him, even in an oblique way, about Román and the car, his immediate response was another question.

"Do you object to having him there?"

"No. I'm just not used to it."

"He doesn't behave badly, does he?"

"Oh, no. He never makes any noise at all. I've often wondered if he isn't bored to the point of stupefaction, though."

"I've never heard him complain. But to answer your question, in this society, it would be awkward for us to go around alone. Román makes it all right."

And that's as far as we got. That word, awkward, would appear more than once in the future, and was used by him to tighten the reins on any situation which seemed to be slipping out of his control.

One afternoon we went on a surprise visit.

"My sister, Luisita, Román's mother, wants us to come for a cup of coffee. Would you like to?"

"Of course. I've never been in a Costa Rican home."

Luisita's house faced on a quiet square across from a church, La Soledad (the Church of Solitude). We stepped directly from the sidewalk into a tiled hall which ran down the center of the house. The hall ended in a large, airy family room with windows across the widest wall, the dining room on one side and the kitchen behind. To the left of the entrance hall was a study, on the right a dark, heavily curtained parlor full of unyielding furniture designed to give you a pain in the small of the back; fortunately, the room was only used for funerals and other rituals.

Luisita turned out to be exactly opposite from Pepe. She was witty. She was full of fun. She was an outrageous mimic to whom no one was sacred. Talking all the time, she invited us into the dining room and seated us at a table with a cloth down to the floor, silver dishes filled with cakes and cookies, and some of the best coffee this side of heaven. Her delicate face with its black eyes and finely chiselled features looked like an Iberian cameo. Sitting down and then immediately standing up, she served us everything, ordered the maid around, introduced her older son, Arturo, and expressed delight at entertaining a lady friend of her brother's—a man she obviously adored but considered a bit weird.

As we came down the entrance hall past the grim parlor I saw another statue of the Heart of Jesus, graphic and bloody, a small candle burning before it. Just to keep the conversation going, Pepe asked who the priest was at the church across the street, and Luisita answered with the name of someone who had been at school with him. Later, after she and I became friends, she told me that though she was a devout Catholic she only had two children and never intended to have any more.

"I use something, but because that's a mortal sin, I go to confession every Sunday, and I admit to the priest what I'm doing. He orders me to repeat a certain number of Hail Marys, I'm forgiven for my sin—and then I go home and do the same thing again."

As Luisita explained it, she was unwilling to have any more children, but was equally unwilling to challenge her church openly, so she felt comfortable with the compromise she'd been able to devise.

* * * * * * * *

After that Pepe and I went on visits to his family over many weekends. But it took some time for me to realize what it was all about. At first I had thought it was just to show me other aspects of Costa Rican society along with some of its more intimate customs. Since often my aunt and uncle went also, and many of Pepe's business relatives had been clients of the bank, it all seemed friendly and easy with a certain old-home-week familiarity. I hadn't been aware that I was being inspected or that his family was welcoming me with particular warmth. They explained to me later that they were so happy to see me because Pepe was already thirty-five years old, and they felt that it was time for him to settle down.

As sometimes happened during the rainy season, there was a break in the weather. Instead of the rains beginning every afternoon about two o'clock, during these particular days there were clear skies in the morning, and though an ominous overcast covered the skies in the afternoon, there were none of the usual downpours which took place during most of the rainy season. On the first day of this brief respite, the big, blue motorcycle appeared, there was the accustomed rattle at the gate, and Pepe was there.

"We should take advantage of the weather," he announced. "A trip to the Irazú volcano is the best way to do it. Wear a jacket. We shall be going up over eleven thousand feet."

Half an hour later we were rolling through Cartago, a former capital of the country. From there we began the steady climb up and up, on a road which wound around the flanks of the volcano itself, through farmlands so lush and green the scenery looked as though it had been dipped in a vast tub of Impressionist paint. We passed little farm houses nestled into dips and crannies along the flanks of the mountain, gently sloping fields dotted with black and white cattle, and an occasional potato patch with a peasant farmer bent over digging up his crop.

About half way up, at six or seven thousand feet, we stopped at a restaurant. How ugly, I thought, looking at the graceless and lumpy house. How could they build something so hideous in a setting as spectacular as this? But I never expressed any derogatory remarks to local people unless they led the way first; I always felt that they knew better than I how bad conditions were.

We stepped into a large central room which promised not only hot coffee but shelter from the wind—especially welcome because the back seat of a motorcycle is not the warmest way to travel, nor the most comfortable. And the restaurant also provided respite from the deafening sound of the engine, now mercifully stopped. As we went in Pepe gave the cuisine a brief recommendation.

"Their specialty here is a local dish, black beans served with sour cream, referred to in Spanish as frijoles negros con natilla. If you have never tried it, you might like it."

We sat at a window and stared out at the blue-green mountains. In due course the waiter arrived with a tray laden with several small, round plates, and a little basket covered by a folded napkin.

"Here are the black beans. They are ground into a -you call that a paste? As you can observe, they are served with the tortillas from this basket and sour cream. Come, I will demonstrate how they are eaten."

With his swift, sure gestures he spread some of the bean paste on a tortilla, topped it with a dollop of sour cream and passed it to me. The contrast of the black and white food was as artistic as a pen-and-ink drawing, and the taste of the hot beans and the cold sour cream was irresistible. (I was to learn later that he considered any discussion about wine, menus, or the preparation of food as proof of the speaker's superficiality and childishness. The sole purpose of food was to provide strength for working and for problem solving—preferably under his direction.) Now, while I stuffed myself inelegantly, he nursed a little cup of coffee, refusing nourishment of any kind. He stirred his drink slowly, his strange, intense, blue eyes watching me with a detachment that seemed almost scientific. What was the matter? Was I eating too much? Talking too much? Not enough? Were black beans dripping down my chin?

If they were he did not refer to them. After I had finished, he put the remains of my lunch, along with the other plates, on a nearby empty table. Then he served both of us more coffee, began to stir sugar into his, and motioned to the waiter to come and clear things up. He had a way of silently ordering people around, whether they were friends, family, waiters, secretaries, business acquaintances or even passers-by. The blue, X-ray eyes would lock into their target and his hands would make gestures which were graphic and compelling. People moved when he wanted them to.

A little later we walked out to the motorcycle to continue our trip to the top of the volcano. In what was becoming a familiar gesture, he patted the headlight, its metal cone glinting in the sudden afternoon sun. For a second he hesitated, one of the few times I ever saw him indecisive. Then he turned to me.

"I believe we ought to get married. You can think about it on the way up to the top."

He smiled his little pixie smile, slammed the engine into life, and we lurched forward, small stones from the drive spraying out behind us like rounded shooting stars.

As we roared upward and upward, I tried to disentangle my feelings. My experiences with men had been limited to college boys whom one "dated" but with whom one did not "go all the way." Or if a girl did, she would have had her tongue cut out before admitting it. Most girls waited until a ring had been placed on their finger—as for me, it was a fate I had always thought would be some time in the future, which I had planned to postpone for several more years.

But now I was confronting a man who was ready to establish a home and start a family. He was brilliant and gifted and had made a success of an enterprise which was enormously difficult. I admired him and felt that life with him would be fascinating, replete with opportunities which Alabama would not offer. And more than anything else, I did not want to return to Birmingham. The limitations of that racist, religious world were too small to permit the kind of life I longed for.

But did I want to leave home and family and country permanently? Could I face living in a society where I would always be considered an outsider and would even speak the language, however fluently, with a foreign accent? In Costa Rica I knew I would not share with my fellow citizens either a common religion or heritage or the experiences of childhood or schooling—and the knowledge filled me with a vague foreboding.

Without subterfuge or self deception I admitted to myself that I was not attracted to him on an emotional basis. Like many women in their relations with men I was attracted by what he did, what he had accomplished, and perhaps subconsciously by how much power he could command both in the present and what I sensed would be his in the future. I did not pretend to him or to myself that I was in love with him. Once, when I had said as much, his answer had been the classic one voiced throughout the ages.

"You will fall in love with me later, and anyway, I love enough for two."

Perhaps he was right. Inexperienced as I was I sensed that a permanent relationship founded on "being in love" seemed somewhat shaky. I had watched too many friends in love today and out tomorrow. For some time I had wondered why la gran passión was always offered as an excuse for making some of life's most irrational decisions. His approach just might be more intelligent.

We reached the top, left the motorcycle on the side of the road, and walked over to the rim of the volcano. Though there had not been an eruption since the last century, the Irazú smoldered and smoked like a gigantic engine. When the wind blew the white vapor away, bright yellow patches from sulphur deposits flamed along the walls of hardened lava which spiralled down and down into a

66

brilliant emerald-green pool at the bottom of the crater. I stared down into the steaming clouds, mesmerized and a little frightened while the words of MacBeth's witches echoed through my mind.

"Double, double, toil and trouble,

Fire burn and cauldron bubble."

Was this going to be my fate? Was I linking my life to a man convinced that destiny had picked him for a role as yet unknown who would drive relentlessly towards a future only he would determine? What place was there for me who might not be strong enough to cope successfully with that crushing ambition? Was there any way to know before it was too late?

"Well," he demanded, "yes or no?"

Across the yawning crater the wind pushed against us, cold and unforgiving and so noisy our words were snatched away and driven towards the cloudy horizon.

I tried to stall one more minute.

"Will it be like that?" I asked, pointing down into the seething vapor.

"Marriage to me will probably be much worse," he answered with rare insight, for I had noticed he was not given to groping around in his own soul. "But a young woman is better off with a husband than without.

And I am used to solving problems so I can help you deal with whatever you have to face." He smiled his little half-moon smile and added gently, "including your aunt."

Chapter VI

The wedding was a civil ceremony which probably lasted less than two minutes. Performed by the mayor of San José, a friend of Pepe's who put on her official sash and delivered the words in her office, we had no reception, no champagne, and only two witnesses which the law required. Since I didn't speak Spanish well I hardly understood a syllable of the proceedings and was not sure what I had agreed to—or, indeed, if I had agreed to anything. But for years afterwards, whenever Pepe wanted me to do something, he would try to persuade me by saying that that's what I had promised in the wedding ceremony.

October's torrential rains, called a temporal, had begun. Because Pepe needed to be out in the country, we decided (meaning he decided) to live in La Lucha, the large sisal finca where the rope factory was located. So I changed from my blue wedding dress into a pair of slacks, we packed food and a few clothes into the back of his Dodge, and started across the mountains to begin an unfamiliar and confusing new life.

In those years we would drive out to a little town, Desamparados (the Homeless Ones) and change to horses for the seven or eight hour ride to the finca. That meant that everything we carried had to be packed into saddlebags, so during the rainy season our motto became less is more. The rains had made the roads impassable except for horses or oxen, and even four-wheel-drive jeeps would get bogged down in the mud. When that happened a pair of oxen would be hitched up to the bumper of the jeep so that it could be—ignominiously—pulled out of the morass.

We left the car under the same shed which also housed the stable where our horses were waiting. The rains hammered down so heavily we could hardly see twenty yards. As I walked to my horse, trying to look both masterful and knowledgeable, I saw a stable boy over to one side, holding my capa, my brown rubber raincoat long enough to cover the wearer from the neck down to the stirrups, and with an extra tail which spread over the horse's rump and kept the rain from running down into the saddle. In more or less the same form it was worn in most tropical countries where people rode horseback as a means of transportation. The capa showed me that I could manage rain blowing in my face but not trickling into my fondillo. For some reason, universally understood, sitting in a saddle full of water seemed too harsh a twist of fortune to be accepted.

First, I mounted the horse with what grace I could muster, one stable boy holding the horse still and another helping me climb aboard. Then another man, probably somebody's cousin escaping from the rain, handed me the capa. After I struggled into it, he arranged it over the rump, the stirrups and the front of my saddle, and unless I fell off the horse, I found out that I could ride for hours under a drenching downpour and still not get wet. Lastly, someone passed up my hat. This was a heavy brown felt with a wide brim which I tried to arrange on my head so that the slashing winds wouldn't tear it off. As I fastened the strap under my chin I was reminded of the headgear that the U. S. Cavalry wore in old movies as they galloped up to the fort just in time to rescue the heroes about to be massacred by the Indians.

Pepe lead the way out into the pounding rain which promised to go on forever. I was assailed again by what was becoming a familiar feeling: a wave of astonishment that I was really in Central America, riding a horse along a muddy road towards a sisal farm where I would be living the rest of my life. What was I doing here? How had it all happened? And would it prove a mistake, this marriage to a man whom I both knew and didn't know? What would we do to each other, how could we shift and change and grow until we finally fit—at least enough to make life tolerable? Perhaps like all newly-weds, I was intrigued by the adventure of my new status but consumed by doubts about the wisdom of my decision. Aunt Ernestine had been so sure. Pepe had been so decisive. But here I was living out their vision and painfully aware that uncertainty was holding the reins with a firmer grip than I.

For the moment, though, there was no time to unravel these conundrums. I had to keep upright on a horse during a journey which would last more than nine hours. Most experienced riders would make the trip in less than one day, but Pepe had realized that I couldn't stand so many hours on horseback, so he had planned for us to put up for the night at a friend's farm. Our honeymoon would be spent in La Lucha, a working-honeymoon during which he would do what he had done for years, ride through the plantations, check on the work, decide where to put in another road, help direct the crews in repairing the canals to bring water down to the small electric plant and to the rope-making machines, and figure out where to build other houses for the workers living on the farm.

The rainy season in Costa Rica lasts from May or June to the last days of November, the tons of water getting heavier and heavier as the weeks move along. We had married towards the end of October, and so were facing the worst part of the rains. People in Costa Rica rarely start on a horseback trip in weather as bad as ours, but we had to arrive in La Lucha about noon of the following day. We were carrying the payroll for several hundred workers living on the farm who needed their wages to buy food for the coming week.

The driving rain beat noisily on the peaked top of my hat and slid off in sheets from the wide brim protecting my face. The horses' hooves made a clopping sound as we trotted along, for the road was hard surfaced near the town, but would soon become a twisting, single-lane trail the farther we retreated back into the countryside. Coffee fincas spread out around us, mixed with small peasant farms whose little patches of black beans and potatoes faded off in the distance.

"We shall stop in about two hours and have coffee," Pepe comforted me, probably wondering himself what he was doing here with a new wife who could barely ride a horse and still spoke his language imperfectly. "We should proceed as fast as we can now because soon the road will get worse, and we shall have to continue at a walk."

The miles began to roll away. We were the only travellers along the winding road, not even oxcarts were willing to face the downpour. For a little while the road was almost flat but after a short distance the incline started, and the ever-present mountains seemed to move closer, slowly coming to meet us. People who had travelled in Europe often said that Costa Rica looked like a tropical version of Switzerland, and now, seen through the incessant downpour darkened by ominous clouds, the landscape took on an unreal quality as though it were the backdrop for a play.

With no permanent damage I survived the jolting ride, the primitive food in the peasants' house along the way, and the night in a room where fleas were plentiful, the hospitality gracious, and the absence of electricity, hot water, and indoor toilets no longer surprising. Our breakfast was black coffee and tortillas. Pepe and I always spoke English so that he could practice and so that I wouldn't sound like an idiot. When I asked if there was any milk or cream for the coffee he stared at me in silence for a moment.

"No, there is not. Milk is a fragile commodity which requires extreme cleanliness, great care in handling, and above all, refrigeration. So it is not often found this far out in the country." I couldn't figure out why but somehow, the way he had delivered the precise explanation made me feel slightly guilty, as though I had requested something bordering on depravity.

We pressed on towards La Lucha, now a mere four hours away. The mountains got higher, the thick clouds darker, and the rain continued unabated. Our horses had been changed for larger, stronger ones, because from now on until we reached La Lucha we would be riding in mud often up to the animals' knees. After a while I got used to the different sounds heard on horseback: the bridle jangled, the saddle creaked, and the rider made a sort of clucking noise to encourage the horse to keep going. Most distinctive were the different sounds of the horse's hooves, almost as sharp and clear as musical notes, and every change in clop and ping struck me as basic material for a peasant song. Riding up a road paved with asphalt produced one sound, on a surface with crushed rock where the hooves were constantly striking large stones another, and in deep mud something different still, a soft, sucking noise as the animal drew his foot out of the sticky mass. I was sure Stephen Foster could have created another Suwanee River with those vibrations.

My horse's name was Santa Clara, a big mare who was soft and calm, and who could hardly be anything else with the deep mud we were struggling through. I found myself talking to Clara, asking her to be careful. "Please don't fall down, Santa. Please don't throw me off. It'll be so humiliating! I'll give you—what? Sugar? Some carrots? What the hell did horses eat as special treats?" Pepe had said that after a horse had been ridden for six or seven hours, it had to rest for three days to recover its strength. "I'll arrange for you to rest a week, two if you'd like. Just don't fall down."

We were at an altitude now of nearly seven thousand feet. In spite of the heavy woolen sweater I wore under the thick raincoat, it was getting colder. The combination of humidity and wind made our ride increasingly uncomfortable, for we had to proceed at a walk as the animals picked their way along the road. It had been cut to pieces by the oxcarts whose heavy wooden wheels were bound in iron to help preserve them from the wear and tear of the rocky trails. I began to hate everything, the incessant rain, the cold, the mud, the ache in my back, the endless road stretching out forever before us, the lucha sin fin indeed.

Without any warning, my horse suddenly slid in a treacherous place and lunged to one side. Caught off balance, I was thrown forward, my feet sliding out of the stirrups. I clutched wildly at the pummel, the horse's neck, her mane. The world swayed around me as the horse slid again. Letting go completely of the reins now, I felt my clawing hands grab the rough, stiff hair of Clara's mane as I fought to stay in the saddle. Shaking with fear I felt the heavy raincoat dragging me downward. Fleeting pictures flashed through my head of people falling off their mounts, getting tangled in their coats or stirrups, and being dragged for long distances until someone could catch the animal.

Fortunately, my horse had the good sense to stop. I got my feet back in the stirrups and grabbed the reins with one hand, struggling to straighten the raincoat with the other. After a moment, my heart stopped trying to jump out of my chest and the world swung upright again. I gulped in mouthfuls of air, feeling Santa Clara move slowly forward. If I had expected Pepe to ride gallantly up beside me, hold out a steadying hand, and take the reins to help me over the bad places, I was disappointed. He did nothing more than issue a calm order.

"Loosen the reins," he said. "Let the horse go where she wants to. She knows where to step." And then he added, "We shall be there in an hour."

In addition to the rain we now had to confront another antagonist: fog. It came up suddenly, thick and impenetrable, a dark grey presence which blanketed everything, so heavy we could hardly see five yards ahead. Mysterious and eerie, it engulfed us completely, and seemed to soften the sounds of our journey, quieting the jangle of the bridle and smoothing the noise of the horses' hooves. Only the wind was a steady moan as it bent the tops of the trees and continually tugged at our hats and made our raincoats flap up and down.

What a honeymoon trip, I thought. Frightened, now dripping wet from my near fall, and worst of all, saddle weary, I clung to the pommel in front of me, hoping the horse wouldn't slip or stumble again, or that I wouldn't get so tired I'd just give up and tumble off.

As we came to the top of another rise, I thought I heard something up ahead. But the fog closed us in, hiding whoever or whatever was waiting beyond the limits of our vision. After a moment the sound seemed to come again, a metallic clink, muted by the distance.

"Do you hear something?" I asked.

"Yes."

"What is it?"

"You'll see." Since his tone of voice wasn't worried, I relaxed a little and let my horse slosh and suck her way forward through the fog and the deepening mud.

It came again, the jangling sound, and then the stomp of a hoof and a whinny, and more jangling. Suddenly the wind shifted, the fog thinned and began to roll away, and there before us was a group of horsemen, waiting in a wide place in what passed for a road. There must have been about eight or ten of them, all wearing the same long raincoats and wide brimmed hats, some of them smoking as they chatted and laughed and happily ignored the rain. As we moved slowly forward it seemed to me that they all spotted us at the same moment for abruptly the laughter and chatter stopped and they turned their horses to face us, reining them back so we would have what safe footing there was on the slippery trail.

Pepe called out, "Hola, como están?"

A chorus answered. "Hola, Don Pepe. Como está? Y la Señora?"

It seemed to me that they all began to talk at once. "Que tiempo más malo! Como ha llovido, por Diós! Un temporal que no termina. Bienvenidos! Felicidades."

Then one by one each man came forward, removed his hat in spite of the rain, and mumbled something.

"What are they saying?" I asked helplessly. "I can't understand anything!" I felt awful, wondering if I would ever learn Spanish or if I would turn out to be like so many other Americans who moved to a foreign country and couldn't even be bothered to find out how to say please and thank you.

"They are telling you their names, some with four long ones. These are the top men of La Lucha. The big one there is the foreman, and the others are heads of work squads."

"Why don't they shake hands? I thought people here shook hands all the time."

"Not yet. They will when they know you better. After all, you are the señora. If you notice they don't even look you directly in the face. They are very shy." Then he must have seen how tired I was. "It's only another half hour."

We started off, the whole troop of us, jangling and sloshing and slipping along under the hammering rain. Pepe immediately began a conversation with the manager of the farm, the tall, bronzed man he had pointed out as the foreman. Lidio answered questions and kept up a constant stream of observations about the works going on at the farm. Though I couldn't follow much of the talk, it turned out to be my introduction to the endless problems involved with running an agricultural-industrial enterprise, made more difficult by isolation and an almost total lack of communication. The nearest telegraph was two hours away by horseback. Telephones did not reach this far away from the urban centers. During six months of the year the oxcart and the horse were the only means of transportation. Though I found it difficult to believe, I soon discovered that for those living in the country during the rainy season, life moved at the same pace as Cervantes' characters in the 16th century story Don Quijote .

Just as Oscar Wilde's weariest river wound somewhere safe to sea, so we finally started down the last endlessly curving road from the top of the mountain to the stream at the bottom, bound on our predetermined way. And a hundred and fifty yards from the water was my new home. It was not exactly a marble palace for it was the same little house where my aunt and uncle and I had had lunch the first time Pepe had invited us out for a visit. It was made of second class wood and was painted white and blue and dark red because those were the bits of paint left over from other jobs around the farm. In several places the paint was slightly peeling leaving exposed raw wood. Uneven cement steps lead up to a miniscule porch and to a door which slanted to the left, having been warped by the rainy season's humidity. A small living-dining room looked out over the river with a study which measured ten feet by ten opening to one side. Down a windowless passage was the bathroom made of corrugated metal with a diminutive shower so small I could hardly turn around in it. The pièce de résistance was the wooden floor. Its widely spaced boards had been designed by Pepe as a model of efficiency because the water would drain swiftly out and not stand half the day clogging up the drainpipe.

But even after all these years, my clearest memory is of something else. The house had been decorated by the cook, a round peasant woman who laughed easily whenever she said anything to me, a single gold tooth among the other false teeth in her smile. To impress her numerous relatives living on the farm and who constantly dropped in for coffee, she had hung strings of multi-colored wooden beads before each door in the house, even the bathroom. Every time a door was opened or closed, the beads would go clack-clack and get tangled in our clothes or catch in anything we carried.

The day after we arrived Pepe wanted me to listen to him read aloud so that I could correct his pronunciation of English. He had brought a copy of TIME magazine, a periodical he read every week. The idiomatic language irritated him because it was difficult for foreigners to understand, even for one whose command of English was as good as his. But he forced himself to read the magazine nonetheless, knowing that the colloquial expressions were common among people who spoke fluent English. It was soon obvious that he was determined to speak fluently no matter what the cost—for either him or me.

76

Before we began he said, "By the way, if there's anything around the house you would like to change, of course do it."

"It's just those damn beads! They're driving me crazy!"

"What beads?" He asked blankly.

"Those! Over every door!" To my stupefaction, I realized that he hadn't even seen them, not once in all the years they'd been clacking there. "They're so awful! Couldn't we take them down?"

"Perhaps you mean ugly," he corrected me, "not awful. By all means, take them down. Tell Maria, she's the fat one with the gold tooth. But be very polite in speaking to her, or to any of the other servants."

There it was again, that hot jab of guilt. It would never have occurred to me to be harsh or insensitive to the maids. They were so helpless in confronting their employers that to treat them unkindly would have been a form of cruelty I could not even have imagined. But why had he used that tactic again?

Eventually the beads came down. And eventually, we settled into a routine. In the morning our breakfast would be brought up from the kitchen on the lower floor where the maids lived. After the meal, Pepe would read, sometimes aloud but more often to himself. We would sit in his study crammed with the books and journals which flowed over everything, our two chairs side by side. There was only room for two people if they both didn't try to inhale at the same time. Since he liked silence in the morning, we would each have a book, mine usually a Spanish one so that I could build up my vocabulary, his in English for the same reason. The silence would stretch out around us, the only sound the soft turning of the pages. Occasionally he would look up and smile at me, but I was not encouraged to say anything.

Sometimes I would sit there holding the book but letting my mind wander. During certain periods of very bad weather called a temporal, the rain poured down all day in a steady drumbeat, thumping on the tin roof so loudly it was often difficult to talk. Because of the altitude and the dampness, the house was always cold. At night, the low voltage of the electric plant meant that all lights were dim and pale, never giving out a strong enough glow to permit us to read comfortably. It seemed to me that a pervading gloom penetrated everywhere. I would remember Alabama, my brothers and sisters, Sunday dinner with relatives and friends, summers spent in our home up in the mountains of North Carolina, leaves brilliantly colored in the autumn, all of it mixed with music, voices calling to each other, feet pounding up and down the stairs, gargantuan quantities of food to fill up teen-age boys, and my mother's saving sense of humor which lifted everything onto a plateau rocking with laughter.

How different it all was now. Behind a wall of mountains in Central America, mired down in homesickness, I forgot my objections to the Alabama I had fled. Its stultifying repressiveness faded, and instead I revelled in a selective memory which retained only the fleeting, golden moments of my school days, at this distance filled with warmth and light.

One evening when I was shivering, I said, "Wouldn't it be wonderful to have a fireplace! There's so much wood around here that fuel wouldn't be a problem."

"I can design a fireplace," Pepe said.

"I don't know," I said tactlessly. "You have to work out the proportions between the opening of the fireplace itself, and the throat where the smoke goes up. Otherwise, it all comes into the room."

He stared at me for a moment, impressed by my vast knowledge of pyrotechnics. "How do you know that?"

"I told you my father's an engineer. I remember his talking about that once when we visited someone whose fireplace smoked."

"Where would you like it?"

"How about right there between those two windows? And we could put bookcases somewhere, and two built-in benches underneath the windows."

Pepe pulled out the volume of the Encyclopedia Britannica which dealt with fireplaces and buried himself in the article. I, of course, was convinced that the whole project was just a passing fancy. To try to design a fireplace when he'd had no experience with one, and never even lived in a house where one was used, seemed too remote a possibility to take seriously.

But the next morning he got up early and disappeared. While I was still at breakfast, there was a thump on the porch, and noises as someone dragged and bumped heavy objects up the steps, and then the door banged open. Pepe, his clothes covered with mud, was helping four men pull and haul a collection of large stones into the living room. They were followed by other men carrying a collection of lumber, tools, nails, saw horses, and sheets of iron plate—along with a generous collection of mud on their heavy shoes. The rain dripped off their clothes and hats making the mud turn into widening puddles on the floor.

Seeing my startled face, Pepe smiled his little gnomish smile and announced his plans.

"We shall start right away. We shall have this work finished in three days. And then, according to the encyclopedia, it has to dry for two days. But by this time next week, you will have your fireplace."

The hammering and banging and sawing started about a minute later and seemed to me to continue for the next hundred years. Everybody gave opinions and everybody made suggestions about how to do everything, in spite of the fact that no one there had ever seen a fireplace or had even heard the word before the work had begun. It was a project which caught the imagination of the peons who began to talk earnestly about what Don Pepe was building in his living room.

"Has visto? Don Pepe está construyendo un horno en la sala!"

"Pues, claro! La Macha (their name for me) lo está obligando, hombre."

"Bueno, pero está bien porque—yai- que se puede esperar? Los estranjeros, toditos, están completamente locos."

"Completamente, hombre! Ellos pueden caminar chingos, chingos en la calle y nadie les haría caso. Entonces, un horno en la sala para ellos no es nada."

Pepe found the conversation of the workers endlessly amusing. "They're saying that I'm building an oven in the living room. But since all foreigners are crazy, they could walk naked down the street and nobody would pay them any attention, and anyway, the whole thing is your fault".

Suddenly the rain stopped, and we had a few days reprieve. The work went on, carpenters hammered, stone cutters cut, and little by little, the fireplace actually started to take shape. After a few days I began to feel that every person living on the farm had come ostensibly to observe the work and to give advice— when what they really wanted was to see the new señora. They would appear at the door, their eyes round with wonder, and would speak earnestly to one of the maids.

"Donde está La Macha?"

When I came into the room, they stared at me speechless with astonishment. I was the first foreigner most of them had ever seen. They were unused to women who had green eyes instead of black, brown hair instead of dark, and skin which was not brunette. And who couldn't even speak Spanish! Bewildered, they clustered in the doorway, their faces as full of confusion as though they were looking at a giraffe.

And then they began to discuss me with child-like frankness. "Ella no está muy gorda," said the brother of the cook, Herminia.

"Talvez su familia es pobre y no tienen mucho de comer."

"Herminia me dijo que no sabe nada de la cocina, ni hacer tortillas!"

"The most Sainted Virgin! Not make tortillas! Poor Don Pepe. He's going to starve to death."

On one occasion Pepe was in the house and heard their conversation which tended to lack originality once they had established the main theme of the day.

"They're saying that you're not very fat, perhaps because your family was poor and there wasn't much food. And that anyway, you don't know how to cook and cannot even make tortillas."

When the weather was good we would ride out on horseback in the mornings so that Pepe could see the progress of the work of the finca. During most of the rainy season the mornings were dazzlingly clear, the sky arching endlessly above the surrounding mountains and a gentle wind keeping the trees constantly moving. Now I observed with different eyes the farm which he had shown us the first day my relatives and I had visited La Lucha. Because the terrain was so mountainous, the nearly a thousand acres of the finca seemed to cover an enormous chunk of real estate.

By now I was able to find my way around, and though I almost never went out alone, I was becoming familiar with the various buildings on the valley floor. Strung out along the small river were the rope factory, the warehouses, the country store and the shops where the machinery was repaired. Simpler pieces for the spinning and looming machines were made from scratch. On the other side of the river up a steep winding road impassable except to oxcarts and jeeps was a little settlement built around a soccer field which had been hacked out of the surrounding mountains with pick and shovel. On one side was a tiny schoolhouse for the children of the farm, and near that, several more houses of peons who worked in the rope factory. And as far as the eye could see marched the rows of sisal plants on which the whole enterprise depended, the stiff, inflexible leaves standing out from the stem, a tough green exterior covering the tough white interior of long fibers from which rope and agricultural bags were made.

There's a saying in Spanish, "The eye of the master fattens the horse", meaning that if the owner is around, everything moves along more efficiently. Needless to say this owner had the kind of eyes which saw everything and especially the things that hadn't been done as he had instructed. He also had the kind of eyes which bore into you and which made you feel slightly guilty all the time, even if you couldn't explain why. As soon as he glanced in your direction you knew that somehow, some time, some place, you hadn't done whatever it was that you should have done—even if you didn't know what it was you should have done. You just knew that you had failed. He used it automatically on everyone, all the time, and as a technique for controlling people, it was more efficient than any methods developed by the KGB.

* * * * * * * *

By now the fireplace was finished. Made of soft beige, uneven stone, it dominated the small room, and would have been big enough for a salon thirty feet long. Flanked by windows, it had bookshelves built into the sides at right angles to two cushioned love seats, and its heat warmed the whole house. To Pepe's immense satisfaction, it functioned perfectly, smokeless and pure, and he soon pictured himself as the world's most advanced expert in all forms of internal heating. In the mornings he would lay the fire with the precision of someone building the Great Pyramid, every stick of kindling placed with exactness so as to generate the greatest amount of heat. And anyone who came to talk to him, no matter how pressing the business, had to listen to his explanations of how a fireplace functioned. When the foreman would bring people to discuss farm problems with him, Lidio's eyes would roll back with despair as Pepe would launch into a speech about fireplaces including their dangers and technical problems. The discourse always ended with the same observation.

82

"Of course it is inefficient because ninety-five percent of the heat goes up the chimney, but you can compensate for that by its beauty and the sense of home which it conveys."

He never grew tired of the remarks of the peasants who repeated over and over their bewilderment about the changes in Don Pepe's house.

"Have you seen it—the oven in the parlor?"

"Man, but that's nothing! Now he's even putting his books in the oven!"

Little did we know as the fireplace was being finished that we would be able to enjoy the books in the oven for only a few short months before our lives would change forever.

Chapter VII

Every ten days or two weeks Pepe would go into San José to arrange about making payments on loans, having supplies shipped out to the farms, and getting further moneys to keep La Lucha running. These trips of his, requiring seven or eight hours on horseback, and two or three days in town, meant that I was left alone on the finca with no English-speaking people nearer than fifty kilometers. Two maids slept in the house so I was not afraid, but my Spanish at that time was still so rudimentary that I could hardly communicate above the level of 'que día más lindo' and 'por favor, una taza de café.' Though I could read fairly fluently, in speaking I was hampered by my shyness and my general feeling of inadequacy. And further hindered by being married to a brilliant man who spoke my language flawlessly as far as grammar was concerned, and whose vocabulary in most areas was rich and varied.

It was only in intimate domestic matters that he was uncertain. "What do you call that shirt you wear under your dress?" he once asked.

"It's not a shirt. It's a slip."

"There's also a verb, to slip, true?"

"Yes, but this is a noun. Or you can say petticoat."

"How do you know which to say?"

"Petticoat is usually longer and fuller."

"Fuller? Fuller of what?"

I had the feeling that in the three months since we had been married we had had dozens of confused linguistic conversations like this. He could discuss the

Second Law of Thermodynamics or some of Spinoza's ideas, but he did not know how to describe the difference among bedroom slippers, dance slippers or ballet slippers—and from an intellectual point of view, he badly wanted to be able to distinguish among them.

I found out later that in addition to business meetings, he was increasingly involved with politics, though still in a peripheral way. After office hours he would have dinner with, or speak on the phone to a widening circle of friends and relatives. The worsening political situation absorbed his attention more and more, as it did with a growing number of people. He was outraged at the corruption in government offices where nothing was done unless you were either a friend of the worker or else passed over a bribe. Services of all kinds gradually slackened. Streets and highways became impassable, hospitals and clinics worked shorter hours, the country's one university began cutting back on classes.

In a small country, corruption of government officials cannot be hidden. 'The government' is not something two thousand miles away in Washington; it is right there across the park. The Minister of Public Works probably played soccer with you; the Chief Justice of the Supreme Court was in your law class. If one of them suddenly moved into a palatial house or started giving lavish parties with his wife dressed in imported French gowns, you knew about it. And so did everyone else.

Like so many other people in the country, the more Pepe learned about what was happening throughout the nation, the angrier he became.

As usually occurs with a new administration, the government of President Calderón Guardia began in a warm glow of hope. A beloved physician, he was perceived as a man of compassion and kindness to whom people could turn when they faced problems they were incapable of solving for themselves. He would get a father out of jail, find a job for a husband, provide a house for the homeless, bring a child into the hospital for an operation. And at the beginning of his administration, he did all that and more; as long as problems were on an individual, personal scale, he provided a few solutions.

But soon the difficulties he faced became too large. Though he probably liked solving everyone's problems, he finally realized that they were too complex for his piece-meal approach and that something along a national effort was necessary. Somewhat foggily, he became aware that social legislation on a wide scale needed to be passed to protect workers; at a minimum they must have a wages-and-hours law, unemployment compensation, and health benefits. In other words, a Social Security system was indispensable. The country needed more schools, more teachers, more playgrounds, more roads opening up the rural farming areas, more support for cultural institutions. In short, the endless demands of a growing society stretched away into the distance and to satisfy them required support from the Congress and from large segments of the population.

Since Calderón came from the moneyed elite, in the early months of his administration he received considerable support from the wealthy, land-owning class, the large finqueros. They had been at school with him and in many cases had been treated by him on a professional basis, so their relations were close and personal. But as the months passed and his administration settled in, many of his social programs, with their protection for the workers, began to impinge on the privileges of the wealthy. Gradually their enchantment with him started to wane. More and more they used against him the ancient cry, Es un traidor! a traitor to his class.

He was not so much un traidor to his class as a politician who could read the numbers. Though he had little grasp of public administration or of how to organize a government, he came to the conclusion that there were more of the little people than of the wealthy, and that therefore his greatest political support would be found among the workers and the peasants. But that meant that they must continually be wooed with further social programs which cut more deeply into the privileges of the wealthy—which turned them more and more against

86

him, further eroding his support on the political front. As that process continued, Calderón began to look about for other allies.

He found two of the most unlikely colleagues.

As Uncle Vinell had told me earlier, the founder and leader of Costa Rica's Communist Party was an unusual man named Manuel Mora. He was a staunch ideologue and a True Believer but also a practical politician. Realizing that Calderón needed support, he offered his party's help in exchange for social legislation to protect the working class. Though his party was not large it was well organized and was able to command attention because its leaders had learned something about manipulating public opinion. Calderón accepted Manuel Mora's proposal of assistance and the two men became collaborators.

The third member of the strange triumvirate was the Archbishop of Costa Rica. A highly intelligent man from peasant beginnings, Monseñor Victor Sanabria had gone into the church, worked his way up and had been named Archbishop not long before Calderón became president. Because of his background, he was sympathetic to the needs of the peasants (who made up fifty per cent of Costa Rica's population), and was disposed to help them in other ways besides saving their immortal souls. When he realized Calderón's political predicament and listened to his promises about social programs, he agreed to join Mora in what they both hoped would be a national effort at economic reform.

One of the most famous photographs to appear during Calderón's years in office was published at this time. It was a picture showing three men sitting in a jeep. They were Archbishop Sanabria, the head of the Catholic Church, Manuel Mora, the head of the Communist Party, and Calderón Guardia, the head of the Costa Rican government. They sat together, smiling into the camera, on their way to inspect a government housing project which they all supported. The photo created a sensation. The picture of the Archbishop sitting beside the Communist leader, whom most Costa Ricans considered the anti-Christ, seemed to the staunch Catholic majority of the country a betrayal of their collective faith.

Pepe would return from his trips into San José in a rage which mounted steadily as the months passed. He did not object to policies which protected working people or gave them much-needed economic support. It was the idea that friends of the president and his henchmen were getting rich off government contracts, that public funds were going into private pockets when the country needed so many schools and roads and health clinics, that men who were incompetent and corrupt were being appointed to important government positions—these were all public matters which became a form of personal offense to him.

And he was determined to do something about it.

We discussed what to do. Television was still ten or twelve years away, so he had to devise other means of communication. He considered writing a series of articles for the newspapers. Then he thought of holding several public meetings where national problems could be discussed. Or a third possibility was to organize a single, block-buster conference where he would speak as well as one or more of the country's leading political pundits.

"Each course has its advantages and disadvantages," he said." I hope I am not so angry that I won't be able to speak coherently when it's my turn to speak."

Incoherence was not exactly a characteristic anyone ever associated with him. I realized, however, that rage could bring about twisted behavior in anyone, so perhaps his wariness was not misplaced. In all the years we lived together, though, I never saw him express anger unless it was for a purpose; he used it only to pressure people into doing what he wanted rather than a release for his own feelings.

"Nobody will do anything! Nothing!" he added. "At least, nothing dramatic enough to galvanize people into action."

"What about a talk on the radio?" I asked. "Every country store and every bar has a radio. You'll reach more people that way than any other."

He liked the idea and we began to discuss what he should say. He wanted to present a reasoned analysis of some of the country's problems. But I suggested a different approach.

"I think you ought to be careful and not let it run on too long. I know everybody here talks a lot and they can stand longer speeches than in the U. S., but you still have to watch the clock. And how about a little touch of humor? You know how Ticos make fun of everything. And maybe you should include a dramatic flourish or two?"

Though he listened I sensed that he was not taken with the prospect of verbal pyrotechnics. He seemed to want to be low-key, to sound responsible and rational, and to convince people that the situation was serious enough so that some action—based on the country's legal framework—was indispensable.

The months passed. From time to time he worked on his speech which became a kind of joke between us, his magnum opus which he would deliver some day in a mythical, remote future.

In the meantime I continued to learn Spanish. I tried to memorize words as I looked around a room or walked along the roads in the sisal plantation. But out in the country my attempts to learn to speak properly were hampered by the fact that no one would correct me. The workers themselves had only a shaky grasp of Spanish grammar, and even if they had been encyclopedias of knowledge, for them to tell the boss's wife that she had made a mistake would have been unthinkable. Once when I asked the maid if the word for house (casa) were masculine or feminine, she stared at me for a stupefied moment and then gave the wisest possible answer. "Lo que Ud prefiera, (whichever you prefer) Señora."

In learning a new language the unwary can often be trapped by words which sound the same in two languages but which have entirely different meanings. At my sister-in-law's house I explained to a roomful of people that I was embarasada at not speaking Spanish more fluently. When they looked slightly baffled, the English-speaking ones among them explained that what I had said was that I was pregnant at not speaking more fluently. Embarasada means embarrassed in a very special way.

We had been living in La Lucha for about nine months when a major change in our working conditions occurred. After years of pressuring, pleading, threatening and begging, the landowners in the areas around La Lucha had finally persuaded the phone company to install a telephone system. That meant that all the farms owned by our firm could be connected. In addition, the four country stores could be in constant touch not only with each other but with the wholesalers in San José. Furthermore, all the small outlets where La Lucha's rope and bags were sold could be hooked into the system to arrange for deliveries. Finally, the homes of the three Figueres men, Pepe, Brother Antonio, and father, Don Mariano, could all be linked together, though that was left until all the other work had been completed.

From the perspective of today's computerized world it is difficult to picture the problems of working in almost complete isolation. During the rainy season, the only way to get a message from one place to another was to send a man on a horse for two hours through the mud to the nearest telegraph station. He would wire a few lines which usually arrived after a delay of several hours, lines which at best would be slightly garbled or at worst, incomprehensible. So to have a phone with its theoretically instant communication seemed almost a miracle—in spite of the fact that often contacts were uncertain because the operadora wasn't on duty to connect one teléfono to another or because the líneas had been blown down by the wind.

One afternoon about four o'clock I was reading before the fire when the new phone rang. It was Uncle Vinnel. His voice was as controlled as always, but it faded and skittered along the line, now louder and now softer. In spite of the interference I sensed that something was the matter.

"There must be a mistake," I said. "The line's so bad I can't hear. What did you say?"

He tried again, but his voice grew weaker half way through.

"Talk louder," I bellowed into the phone. "It sounds as though you're saying that Pepe's been put in jail!"

"He has been! He made a speech .... over the radio, and the police ...." Static and strange noises, screeches and a high wailing moan cut off the rest. Then the last part of his words..."come into town at once! He's asking for you."

A click and the phone was dead. In jail! How ridiculous! I knew at once that I had misunderstood. People like us didn't go to jail. People like us spoke to the judge, or put up bail, or had our lawyers arrange things. It was insane that my husband could be put in jail! I was outraged at the very thought. And then I began to remember the stories I'd been hearing these last months about the increasing repressiveness of a government which seemed to be slipping out of control. People arrested for criticizing the government. People jailed because they disagreed with policies which seemed to them unjust. Newspapers threatened with having their newsprint curtailed. Radios warned not to be too critical....

Frightened and shaky, I went down to the office of the farm to ask if there were a truck going into town. Or a car which could drive me at least up to the place where our farm road joined the Pan American Highway five kilometers away. Once at the entrance gate I might be able to hail a passing truck or even one of the rickety buses which wheezed up and down the highway going to settlements along the main road between San José and the Panamanian border. From the gate it was only about an hour's drive into the capital and my uncle's house where I could get news about developments.

Workers were loading a truck with rolls of rope for the warehouse in San José.

"Buenas tardes," I said, for even in moments of crisis Costa Rican peasants were formal and polite.

"Señora, buenas tardes. En que podemos servirle?"

Was he asking how he could help me?

"El camión—es el camión—va a San José?" It always took me a few seconds to rearrange the sentence to suit the Spanish construction, and I never knew if what I was saying was what they were understanding.

I thought the driver of the truck said that it would probably be an hour before we left, but I wasn't sure. Whenever I got nervous or frightened or angry, my brain stopped functioning as far as Spanish was concerned and I rarely understood what was being said. But now I grasped the fact that the driver would stop on his way out to pick me up and that we would be in town before the end of the day.

Back at the house I separated the logs in the fireplace so the fire would burn itself out, and put a few things into a bag for my stay in town. Then I called the maid.

"Por favor, una taza de café." I wanted to say please bring the coffee as soon as possible, but I was too nervous to forge the construction of 'as soon as possible.'

This was something Pepe usually did before he went anywhere. I had learned that coffee was always ready on the wood stove. The maid would appear with small cups and saucers on an oval metal tray, a spotless napkin under the saucers, the jet black coffee already served and sometimes even with sugar in it. And we usually sipped a few mouthfuls before doing almost anything.

"La señora va para afuera?" the maid asked, setting the tray down on a table. They always described any trip out of the finca as going outside.

"Si, pero no por mucho tiempo."

As I stirred my coffee before the dying fire I felt the waves of panic rising. What was happening? Why that terrifying sentence from my uncle about the police and Pepe's going to prison? Not to understand clearly made everything more frightening, especially when I remembered reading about people's disappearing inside those impenetrable walls and not coming out for years. Of course, Costa Rica prided itself on not doing anything like that to its citizens. Or rather, it had formerly prided itself on being the one country in Latin America where respect for human rights was a model for the rest of the continent. But now....

The horn of the truck interrupted my thoughts. I said good-by to the maids, picked up my bag and closed the front door. There was no way to know that I would not return for over two years.

Chapter VIII

As long as I live I will hear the clang of the metal door closing behind me as I started down the passage to Pepe's cell. A few steps ahead the guard slouched along, his figure indistinct in the dim glow of bare light bulbs hanging from the ceiling. Patches of faded green paint had peeled from walls which moisture had turned slick and cold; underfoot, the floor was gritty with dirt. The fetid air clung slimily to our cheeks, so heavy with the smell of urine and rotting food I found it hard to breathe.

The passage rounded to the left and there he was, alone in a cell block which should have held twelve men. He was sitting on his bunk, not moving, head down, staring at the floor. I got the impression that he had been sitting like that for a long time. He was dirty, his chin dark with a two-days growth of beard. It made him look menacing and dangerous, and I was aware that I had never seen him really dirty. Almost obsessively clean, he would wash and scrub if he had done anything around the sisal farm to soil his clothes. As I approached the iron bars separating his cell from the passage, I seemed to be confronting a stranger.

Then he heard us and looked up.

The guard spoke suddenly with the rasping voice of a chain smoker.

"Diez minutos," he said, "es todo lo que tienen!" After his announcement that we had ten minutes he stepped back one pace. All during the visit, though, he stood close enough to prevent me from passing over a weapon if I'd been so inclined, his eyes, wary and watchful, never leaving our faces.

Slowly, as though in pain, Pepe got off the bunk and came towards the bars separating us. Why was he walking like that? Had they mistreated him? Beaten?

Tortured even? My stomach turned over. With his dirty fingers he grasped the metal rails closing off his cell and I put my hand over his.

"How did you find out?" he asked.

"Uncle Vinell phoned me at La Lucha. I came into town last night."

We stared at each other for a moment, unable to accept the fact of his imprisonment. Maybe it was all something in my imagination. Maybe we were really at a play or a movie about a man falsely condemned to jail, and we would soon be leaving the theater. It was impossible that I could be married to someone who had actually been picked up by the police and taken to prison. In a family like ours, this kind of thing was unthinkable, simply couldn't happen—unless Fate had made the two of us into a different sort of family, in a different sort of place, with different reasons for being imprisoned, and I would have to accept the consequences.

His voice, petulant and weary, pulled me back. "I wish you had brought some coffee. It gets cold in here at night and they only give me water."

"They wouldn't let me. Alberto Marten arranged for me to see you on condition that I didn't bring in anything....Did they—I mean, did they do anything to you?"

"No. Somebody hit me in the head when they dragged me into the police car—after the soldiers came to the radio station and cut off the broadcast. But nothing else."

I noticed that his electric blue eyes looked faded and watery. Had he been crying? In this place how could he not—the loneliness, the smell—how could anyone remain sane for long?

"What are people saying? Is there any thing in the papers?"

"Everybody's saying everything. The papers are full of it. Pictures of you, of the radio station, of the car that brought you here."

95

"What does Alberto say?" Alberto Marten had handled Pepe's legal affairs as long as he had been in business, and a man with whom he had had endless discussions about political and social problems. A friend of rock-like integrity, Marten was something of a Puritan, incapable of dishonesty, fiercely dedicated to the Majesty of the Law and with a tendency to condemn the slightest breach of behavior which deviated from what he considered correct. With his black, mocking eyes, his voice often full of contempt and his profound knowledge of the law, he was a formidable opponent, and now in Pepe's defense was being his most challenging and aggressive.

"He's starting legal action this morning against the government. His office is getting the papers ready now."

I hesitated a moment and then said, "He says there're rumors you're going to be sent into exile."

Pepe slowly took his hands off the bars of his cell and glanced away. Then half turning, he sagged against the iron rails, suddenly looking so tired I wondered if he would be able to keep on his feet during the rest of my visit.

"Where are they sending me?"

"Nobody seems to know. They probably haven't even decided yet themselves." The guard shifted a step or two to one side and the dirt scrunched under his feet as he scratched himself and then lit a cigarette. In the quietness, the rasp of the match was the only sound. For a little while there was nothing to say. The threat of the approaching exile had made speech impossible, for Pepe had not been out of the country since he had returned from working and studying in Boston and New York twelve years before. And the prospect of not being able to return home whenever he wanted to seemed to crush all life out of him. How long would it last? Where would they send him?

When I couldn't bear the silence any longer I said, "Why do you think they did it?"

"Put me in jail? Who knows? Perhaps they merely panicked. Mine was the first speech with the suggestion that the president should leave office. They may have been so frightened they reacted irrationally." When he spoke again his voice was whiny. "Why didn't you bring me some newspapers?"

"I tried to, but the police took them away."

"Isn't Alberto coming? Or Chico?" His other oldest friend, Chico Orlich was his former business partner and the man with whom he had shared the years in Boston and New York.

"You're being held incommunicado. Nobody can come. Alberto tried to persuade them to let him see you but they wouldn't. I'm the only one they've let in."

The guard suddenly spoke. "Dos minutos más."

Two minutes! How could we say anything in that length of time?

"I think they're going to let me come back tomorrow. Maybe Alberto can arrange for me to bring you clean clothes." Neither of us mentioned exile again, but it hung there between us. Suppose I returned the next day and he had already been sent somewhere else. How could we persuade them to let us know where he was? Would he be taken to the frontier of Nicaragua and just dumped out on the road? Or left somewhere in the jungles of Panama? The idea of exile was so bizarre for an American that the very concept was hard for me to grasp. To be put on a ship or a train against your will and sent across a border to live without resources or friends—how could a government do that to its own citizen whose only crime was to disagree? I didn't know it at the time, but as the years passed, I was to become acquainted with several people, not just men but women and children too, who had been stripped of everything they possessed and sent off to other countries to survive as best they could—often reduced to selling tortillas on street corners in a strange city.

Without warning, the guard stepped forward so that he almost came between us.

"OK, ya! Vamos!" He began moving towards the passage leading to the exit, then stopped to wait for me.

What was there to say? It was all so unreal—the cell block, the dirty mattress whose grey and white stripes had faded beneath years of sweat and stains, our own helplessness—I couldn't seem to grasp any of it. That this little man with his smelly, wrinkled clothes, a damp cigarette sagging from one side of his mouth, had complete control over us was so humiliating I could feel myself shrinking as he lounged towards the door.

"I'll be back tomorrow, as early as they'll let me." I turned to go, wondering if he would be there when I came back, wanting to say something to comfort him but feeling my throat close up too tightly to speak. He still leaned against the bars, forlorn and inarticulate, watching me walk away, my feet scraping along the dirty passage.

Just before I turned the corner of the passage he called out. "When they send me somewhere, will you come?"

"Of course! Of course, I will!" I started back towards him but the guard's voice stopped me.

"Bueno! Que carajo! Vamos! Que pasa?"

I moved away and didn't look back. I couldn't have seen anyway because my eyes were full of tears.

* * * * * * * *

As I was dressing early the next day to go again to the prison, the phone rang. It was Alberto Marten.

"I just got a call from the Security Police. They've taken Pepe to the airport. He's being sent on a special plane to San Salvador."

"San what?"

"The only thing he asked was that they let you join him there."

"Wait! Wait a second! Here, talk to my uncle!" I handed the phone to Uncle Vinell. Like the careful banker he had always been, he had placed a special note pad and pen near the telephone in order to take down the names and phone numbers of everyone who was calling about Pepe. The calls had poured in from the moment the news about him had begun to spread through the countryside. People in the most distant villages had heard his broadcast saying that the political situation was so desperate that the president should resign and let the vice president take over. And then listeners had been shocked by the interruptions—sounds of sirens and police whistles, the security forces charging into the radio station, the shouts and curses and smashing furniture as the government's Special Detail had broken doors and shattered windows—just before the broadcast had been cut off. By a coincidence, a newspaper photographer was having coffee right near the radio station and had been able to snap a series of graphic shots.

Uncle Vinell was holding the phone against his ear. Every now and then he said "Yes, I understand." And then after a moment, "Yes, that sounds reasonable." And then more talk from Alberto. Another little while passed, Uncle Vinell's voice sounded as though the conversation were winding down as he said thank you several times, and wrote a number on the pad beside Alberto's name. Then he hung up and turned to me.

"What? What's happening? Where is he? Where's San Salvador? I know it's north of here, but where?"

My uncle made a soothing gesture.

"Let's take it slowly. First, Pepe is probably leaving right this minute from the airport for the capital of El Salvador, a little country just north of Nicaragua. It will be exile for several months —maybe years—who knows how long. Secondly, the government has given permission for you to join him as soon as your papers are ready. Thirdly, you must go to see Don Antonio—"

"I know. Pepe's brother. He runs the coffee place, Santa Elena. Go on!"

"Don Antonio is getting money for you. That way, you will have something to live on until they can make more careful arrangements, i.e. set up letters of credit or bank accounts. I'll begin making your airline reservations. You'd best start packing."

I took down my suitcases, the same grey ones with the red stripe around the top which I'd brought when I first arrived in Costa Rica. Staring down into the open bags I wondered how you packed for exile. Would the weather be hot or cold? Would you be gone months or years? After prison in one country, did prison await you in the next? I remembered a line from a movie about people trying to get a visa during the Second World War to escape from the Nazis and emigrate to the United States. In filling out the endless forms, one of the characters said, "What is my profession? Waiting." Was I going to spend the next years of my life waiting for my husband to get out of one prison and then go into another?

Since we kept city clothes in town I filled one of the suitcases with his things and one with mine. Then I stood at the window and listened to the old refrain running around my head: what am I doing here, packing to join my husband in exile in a country I'd hardly ever heard of? El Salvador, The Savior, was—my thoughts were interrupted by Uncle Vinell who stood in the door.

"Your plane leaves at three this afternoon. Antonio will send a cable to the hotel where Pepe will be staying, telling him your flight number. The trip is about two and a half hours, because you stop in Managua."

"How do we know where he is?"

"Alberto was called by the Security people with the name, El Gran Hotel. If, for any reason, Pepe and you miss each other at the airport in San Salvador, just go to the hotel and wait. He'll come there."

I began to worry. If we missed each other, if I couldn't find the hotel, if I found the hotel and he didn't turn up, if—if—if. What a leap in the dark! Alone in a country where I knew no one, could only speak Spanish imperfectly and where a repressive government not noted for its respect for human rights was in power, how much help could I expect in locating a husband just sent into exile?

Uncle Vinell saw my distress and tried to be consoling.

"Now don't be upset," he instructed, with about as much warmth as someone helping a teller track down a mistake in tallying her deposit sheet. "It's going to be all right." I must have still looked forlorn because he seemed to become panic-stricken at the prospect of having to express his feelings about the situation— something no Victorian gentleman could ever permit himself to do. Instead, he began to tap with his pen against the little notebook, working out a complicated set of rat-ta-ta-tas whose rhythm quickened as he tried unsuccessfully to find something else to say.

The silence stretched out between us. I was too emotionally battered to help him out of his dilemma or even to walk away and ask Carmen for a cup of coffee. We might have stood there indefinitely if Aunt Ernestine hadn't bustled towards us. She usually started talking while still in the upper hall, and then she would descend clack, clack down the stairs, her high heels smacking sharply on each step. Now she came towards me with a little crystal bottle which glittered slightly as she presented it to me.

"Here, you'll need this. I was going to give it to you anyway for your birthday. Take it for the trip."

As my hand closed around the small, fragile bottle I thought that the one thing a woman needed as she faced an indefinite exile was perfume. I sniffed it and the enticing, exotic scent seemed to sweep around the room, not a fragrance I thought my aunt would ever buy. And just as she proved to be correct in one prediction about Pepe, so now with the perfume she turned out to be right also: I used it as a talisman to help lighten my blackest hours when exile proved to be lonely to the point of hurting.

We had our final lunch together, then Carmen carried my suitcases out to the car.

"Put them there in the back seat," my aunt ordered. "No, not like that, standing up. La Nina (meaning me) will sit back there."

I wedged myself in beside the valises, and we started for the airport, my heart getting heavier and heavier as I faced a future so uncertain I felt almost paralyzed with fear.

"Do you have the money?" Uncle Vinell asked. "Your passport? Your visa?" I nodded. "Where's the money?"

I patted my front, while he looked modestly away. Tucked into my bra were five hundred dollars in cash, a sum which seemed to me enormous, and which only added to my fears. Suppose someone robbed me on the trip! Then Pepe and I, if we ever found each other, would be completely bereft. And if we didn't find each other. . . .! Retreating behind a wall of silence, I sat in my corner of the little black Morris Minor car which my relatives had owned for nearly fifteen years. My aunt was at the wheel, and I watched as the large white flower at the front of the navy hat she always wore while driving swayed and bounced with her erratic chauffeuring. Bumping and jolting over the potholes in the streets of San José, which were perennially in need of repair, we made our way to the airport.

We had of course arrived too early, both my aunt and uncle being compulsively punctual. The plane was still being serviced with mechanics crawling like large beetles around the tail section and over the cowling. Clerks stood behind counters waiting to start banging down their blurred stamps on passports as officials joked with each other before it was time to start checking exit visas.

I was exhausted from the strain of the last few days and began to feel that I had forgotten how to talk. Nothing would come out, no trivial remark about the weather, no question even about the country where I was going. I just sat huddled in a seat so uncomfortable it made my back ache and hoped I wouldn't start crying. Even my aunt for once was silent. Pepe was the first person to be exiled from Costa Rica in this century and the experience had been such a shock, no one knew what to do.

Finally, Uncle Vinell said, "It's a good idea in a crisis just to do the next thing that has to be done. Feed the baby, make the bed, fix the car. Now the next thing to do is stand in line over there to have your papers checked, and you'll be first on the plane."

I stood in line. And eventually it was time to go—though, of course, it was all happening to someone else. Not to me. Feeling wooden and helpless and still unable to talk, I hugged my relatives, shook hands for the second time with some strangers whom I had just met and would never see again, and walked out to the plane. Like my wedding trip with a saddle full of water, here was another twist of outrageous fortune, but this time with no protective raincoat, no sense of Pepe's all-knowing control, just unanswered questions leading along an unchartered road.

Exile had begun.

Chapter IX

My plane was several hours late arriving in San Salvador. Whether it was engine trouble or weather trouble I can't remember, but even before I stepped off the ramp I saw Pepe. Almost speechless with relief, I felt weak enough to have difficulty walking; it made me realize how I had been haunted by the fear of missing him and finding myself alone in a foreign country with no contacts and nowhere to turn.

For him the intervening hours had provided enough of a respite to allow for recovering his forces. Now he looked the way he always did, spanking clean, blue eyes X-raying everything around him as his controlled, economical gestures added to his air of command. The days and nights in prison when he had been beaten by circumstances he couldn't dominate had already been left behind, and I never heard him refer to them again. I sensed that they were a time of such humiliation he wanted only to push them down into the depths of the past where they would be overlain with later triumphs.

I did not know it then but some time between his leaving the prison in 1942, and his arrival in San Salvador he had made the decision to start a revolution. During those hours he had not had time to formulate any specific plans; neither did he have any experience in the matter. He certainly did not know that the arms would have to be purchased in Mexico and that the operation would involve bribing Mexican officials up to the Cabinet level. All he knew was that an armed revolt was the only solution to Costa Rica's political problems—whatever the cost in money or lives. And for the next six years he dedicated himself with single-minded intensity to bringing about the desired result.

Now in San Salvador we established ourselves in El Grán Hotel (a building which many years later was destroyed by fire). Since we had come down three thousand feet from San José, our new home seemed not only suffocatingly hot but because of the abrupt change in altitude, the air itself was so oppressive and heavy it hung about us like a smothering shroud. Our hotel was in the center of town. Although it was the largest one in the city, there were no rooms with private baths. Wealthy travellers stayed with wealthy friends or relatives, and those of us who didn't know people had to make do. On each floor of the hotel the single bathroom was carefully hidden. Down a shadowy hall which turned and twisted, the guests fumbled along. Carrying their soap and towels, they went up a few steps and down some others, followed red arrows and cardboard signs which said, BAÑO, and finally groped their way into a dimly lit room. The door of the BAÑO had an ominous squeak but at least it admitted them to the required hardware which looked like the grandfather of all bathrooms and was almost as old.

Pepe hated the arrangement.

"One of the greatest contributions to civilization which the United States has made is to build the bathroom next to the bedroom," he said, after he had wandered around the halls trying to locate some place to take a shower. "It's barbaric, this European custom of making you walk a long distance to find water."

I agreed. And in addition I especially resented El Salvador's heat which I managed to interpret as a personal offense. To be oozing perspiration all the time seemed to me unladylike and just proved that Nature had set out to make my life miserable. Since air conditioning was almost unknown in most of Latin America at that time, frequent bathing was the only way to remain comfortable and that required a supply of cool water—near at hand. So both Pepe and I hated San Salvador for different reasons.

Heat and lack of water to the contrary, he began establishing contacts right away. He called several business people with whom he had corresponded in previous years about the rope business. Then he made appointments to visit coffee farms and bag factories.

"El Salvador is a place where the blessings of the capitalist system are carried to their ultimate extreme," he said. "Fourteen families either own or control everything. I want to see how it operates."

After a few days I asked, "Why are there no well-dressed people on the streets? In Costa Rica, most of the businessmen wear suits. But everybody here is barefooted and their clothes are all patched."

"There's no middle class here. Either you're one of the Fourteen Families or you're hungry. Tomorrow we're going to have lunch with some of the Fourteen."

The car they sent for us was long, black and elegant. Since many of the streets of San Salvador were not paved, the chauffeur had to drive slowly, easing the big automobile around the pot holes in the center of the city. But once out in the country, we could drive faster because a little way beyond the edge of town, the property of our host began. It was a farm of about three thousand acres. Since much of it was planted to coffee, he kept up his own roads to make it easier for his trucks to haul out the crop.

The coffee trees slid past, row after endless row. They looked lush and healthy, their dark green leaves proclaiming tender loving care. As we moved through the plantation, Pepe pointed over to one side of the road.

"The wealth of this country is based on land. And since about ninety-five percent of it is owned by less than five per cent of the population, you can understand some of the things you see around you."

In a small clearing stood several huts—or rather, leaned. They were nothing more than four posts supporting rusted, sheet-iron roofs. Instead of walls, pieces of old blankets sagged on ropes to form the sides of the houses and one or two inner rooms. In front of each dwelling the earth was packed hard forming a kind of porch. Crouching in the corners of the huts, women pushed bits of wood under stoves made of a flat sheet of iron resting on stones. As they nursed their fires, they swayed back and forth to dodge swirls of smoke which drifted around the blanket-walls. Naked children, their hair caked with dust and sweat, played in the ditches beside the huts. It was impossible to escape the contrast of the higgledy-piggledy arrangement of the hovels with the ruler-straight ranks of coffee trees drawn up in military formation marching towards the green horizon.

Looking at the dirt and squalor, Pepe leaned forward and spoke to the chauffeur.

"Where do the people bathe? In this heat they probably need to three or four times a day."

"They cannot. The señor obliges them to pay for their water. It is brought on the truck in large barrels. They are only able to buy a little for drinking and cooking."

Fifty yards beyond the huts on the opposite side of the road, the car stopped before a large black iron gate. As the chauffeur opened the car door, a fair-skinned man stepped forward, flanked by two guards carrying machine guns across their chests. Trying to ignore the machine guns I couldn't help staring for he was the first elegantly dressed person I'd seen since arriving in El Salvador. Was that soft blue shirt silk? And the white linen slacks—surely made by a skilled tailor.

I had a fleeting impression of jewelry and then our host, Raul Cepeda, was welcoming us and waving us towards the house.

"Les agradezco mucho que Uds vinieran a mi casa," he said. "Costa Rica es famoso en América Central por su gobierno tan democrático." He was graciousness itself, flowing and easy, and when he realized that my Spanish was halting, he switched immediately to English, accented but fluent.

"Why do you speak English so well?" I had learned by now to ask that question because most Latin Americans enjoyed being complimented on their command of a language as difficult to pronounce as English.

"Ah, like so many of us here, I went to the United States to study. The University of Tulane, in Nueva Orleans."

We were moving across smooth green lawns bordered by spectacular scarlet and golden shrubs, the colors brilliant against the white walls of a house. It was surrounded by a wide porch where both guards stopped as Cepeda ushered us in. Arches separated the red tiled porch from the garden, all of it straight out of the history books with their pictures of the structures built by the Spanish conquistadores. Thick, thick walls kept out the heat as we made our way into an enormous living room, huge rugs spread under ancient furniture, crystal chandeliers sparkling in the muted light. It was all so authentic and old and above all, rich, I found it difficult to shift from the poverty of the huts outside to this cool opulence.

"When was the house built?" I asked.

"1619. We have from the King of Spain the original papers granting the property to my family. As you are able to see, the walls are formed of hand-made brick, a meter thick—that is over three feet."

The door to the inner part of the house opened and a woman appeared. She was a little older than I, exquisitely dressed, hair newly done, jewels sparkling on fingers, wrists and ears. Doña Margarita Cepeda was type cast for the role, light brown hair, blue eyes, her body getting a little heavy about the middle but still sensuous and attractive. I guessed her dress must be French, it was so understatedly elegant. And the shoes with the stiletto heels were surely Italian.

"Welcome to El Salvador. Is this your first visit here?" Without listening to our response, she motioned us to a section of the room with a round table and chairs so comfortable I wanted to spend the rest of my life slouching in their depth. "What will you have to drink? Scotch? Vodka? Vermouth?"

I hesitated. Since my Presbyterian upbringing had hampered my knowledge of alcoholic beverages, I always had a problem about what to ask for. Whiskey was too strong, vodka gave me a headache. Don Raul helped me out.

"We have wine, very fine, very light. I order from the Rhine in Germany. Perhaps it would please you. And have some of these. Spanish olives. The best in the world."

The two men began to discuss coffee production, now switching to Spanish. Don Raul was well informed both about the problems of producing the crop in El Salvador and about the world market on which his coffee was sold. "Our main problem here is labor. We can't find anyone. "

"But El Salvador is one of the most heavily populated countries in the world." Pepe objected. "This country teems with people. They're everywhere."

"Yes, but you can't imagine how lazy they are. And inefficient. They're no good."

"How much do you pay them?" Pepe already knew the answer because he hadn't been in the country three hours before he began absorbing information about the history, agricultural production, wages, diets, recreation, rainfall, gross national product and the complete absence of any legislation protecting the workers.

"Well, in terms of the American dollar, about twenty-five cents a day. And they're not worth even that."

"Perhaps if you paid them more, they would be more productive," I said.

For a moment he stared at me without answering. I was to discover that he was not only perplexed by my revolutionary suggestion but also by the fact that a woman concerned herself with problems like labor costs.

"But no one here pays any more. It is only the communists who talk about higher wages. Besides, we supply them with a house."

"Yes, we saw them as we were coming in."

Lunch was announced. Standing in front of a long, heavily carved sideboard loaded with food stood three Indian maids. They had black braids down their backs, spotless, hand embroidered uniforms reaching to the floor, and bare feet. As we went into the regal dining room, Pepe, like a polite Costa Rican, greeted the servants.

"Buenos días. Como están?"

The three dark faces, frozen with astonishment, stared at him in silence, wondering how to respond. I had a feeling that no guest had ever taken notice of their presence before and now they didn't know what was expected of them. Helpless, they glanced at the Señora Cepeda.

"Contesten!" she commanded, in a tone of voice no Costa Rican señora would have dared use to a servant because she would have quit on the spot.

Standing motionless, each of the maids then responded in turn.

"Buenos días, señor," they murmured, their voices so soft they were barely audible, their eyes carefully staring at the floor. Hardly breathing, they waited for further instructions.

"Bueno, ahora pueden servir."

As well trained as a military unit, the three picked up heavy silver platters and began to move around the table. They were graceful and quick, and as I listened to the rustling of their starched uniforms, I wondered what would happen if one of them should drop something. Would the señora have their hands chopped off at the wrist or just their fingers from the first knuckle down? Those Indian faces, opaque and expressionless, seemed to reveal nothing except their helplessness.

They were so pitiful, and the distance between them and their employers so vast it was almost as though the two groups did not belong to the same species.

After lunch we went out onto the wide, tiled porch. Cooled by a fountain with blue and yellow Spanish tiles, we sat in heavy shadows cast by a vine trained from the floor to the tiled roof. I watched the green, lacy wall with its scarlet flowers undulate gently in a benevolent breeze, and remembered the blankets strung on ropes in the huts outside the gate. One of the silent maids served coffee from the plantation in front of us. Needless to say, both Pepe and I felt that the brew was not comparable to the fine, high altitude coffee we would have gotten at home. As a second cup was being offered, a guard materialized at the edge of the porch. Silently he waited until Don Raul turned to him, shifting his gun to a more comfortable position.

"Sí? Qué?"

"Señor, uno de los trabajadores quiere hablar con Ud."

"Bueno, pero cuidado."

I watched as a peon appeared, the one who wanted to talk to the Señor. He was small, shrunk in on himself and ill at ease. His clothes were patched and dirty, his trousers held up by a piece of rope, his splayed feet with their broken toenails had never worn a pair of shoes. As he sidled forward accompanied by the second guard, the muzzles of the machine guns swung slowly in his direction like the hands of a clock moving towards noon.

"Quítate el sombrero," the older guard snapped.

The peon snatched his hat off as though it were burning his head, and stood twisting it in his hands.

"Bueno, Juan, qué quieres?"

"Señor, yo quiero su permiso de matar a Miguel." Unbelieving, I stared first at the peón and then at Don Raul, sure that I must have misunderstood. Had he really asked permission to kill someone?

"Pués, que ha hecho esta vez?"

Don Raul's tone was patient, his voice unhurried. He flicked the ashes of his Turkish cigarette onto the tile floor and took a sip of his coffee.

"Señor, he has stolen some of my corn, the little patch I have been growing near my house for my tortillas."

Don Raul seemed to be considering Juan's request. He glanced over at the trees in the coffee field directly in front of the house. He could see that the branches were beginning to sag under the weight of the ripening crop. The berries, about the color and shape of ripe cherries, peeked among the dark green leaves waiting to be picked, all the work having to be done by hand. I had seen enough coffee farms to know that the busiest time of the year was approaching. Then he turned back to the peón.

"Tome," he said, holding out the butt of his long cigarette, "tu quieres terminar esto?"

Juan took a step forward, reaching out a hand for the cigarette. But the barrel of the nearer gun pushed against his stomach and he stopped, his fingers frozen in mid air. At a gesture from the older guard, the young one took the cigarette from Don Raul's hand and passed it over to Juan. He began to smoke it at once, drawing down deep puffs as he waited for the answer to his request.

"Mire, Juan," said Don Raul, "tu tienes que esperar." He went on talking, using the intimate form of address which he automatically switched to in speaking to all his workers, maids, chauffeurs and inferiors. I missed many of his remarks but knew that Pepe would translate for me as soon as we left. The peon listened carefully, nodded once or twice and turned to go, putting his hat back on as he edged away.

"Gracias, Señor."

Our host looked at his wife and pointed to the little pile of cigarette ashes beside his chair. "Tell Lutecia to sweep these up."

As soon as we were in the car on the way back to our hotel I demanded a summing up of Cepeda's remarks to the peon. "You will find it hard to accept the fact that he was speaking seriously. He told Juan that he needed every worker to bring in the coffee crop which was almost ripe so Juan could not kill the other man just yet. But come back in two or three months and they would talk about it again!" We rode on through the rows and rows of coffee trees. They were well fed and laden with fruit, and were so much more carefully tended than the workers I wondered if the peones ever envied the easy life the coffee trees enjoyed. Watching them march past Pepe said, "Did you notice practically everything that family uses is imported? Spanish olives, Scotch whiskey, German wines, Turkish cigarettes, big American cars, universities in New Orleans."

"And her clothes were as expensive as anything I've ever seen. All European."

"Imagine how much coffee Cepeda has to produce and export to keep up that house and to live like that. But of course, if you pay your people twenty-five cents a day, you can live like a king."

Just as we were approaching our hotel, we passed a small procession. A long line of men, marching two by two, shuffled along, their bare feet stirring up dust, their dirty clothes full of patches.

"Oh, look," I said, "their thumbs are tied together. Ask the driver what they're doing."

Pepe leaned forward. "My God, they must be prisoners! There's a guard at the front, and one at the back. See the guns!" He turned to the driver. "Donde están llevando estos hombres?"

"Como veinte-cinco kilómetros recto al norte hay una cárcel, Señor." So there's a prison up there.

"Van a pie?"

"Si, Señor."

"No tiene Ud una idea de porqué los llevan?"

"No, Señor, pero probablemente robaron algo. Casi siempre algo de comer." So they'd stolen something, probably food, the chauffeur said.

The large, sleek car stopped at the hotel entrance as the prisoners shuffled past. Pepe stared after them as we turned into the doorway of the largest hotel in the capital of El Salvador—with no private baths.

"Poor Central America! We're still living in the Middle Ages."

As I met more of the wealthy Salvadorians I was struck by the physical differences between the upper crust and the peones. Many of the land owners were tall and fair skinned, while the peasantry was dark and Indian looking, their smallness probably due to malnutrition. For the most part, the rich were descendants of settlers from the north of Spain who came to the New World in the Fifteenth and Sixteenth Centuries with grants of land from the crown. Many of their descendants, like our hosts at lunch, were still living on the same properties.

We stayed in El Salvador for three months. I didn't know it until later, but some time during our stay, Pepe's resolve about a revolution began to take definite shape in his mind. He had decided that the first step was to start buying arms and that the best place to find them, maybe the only one, was in Mexico. He had convinced himself that there was but one way to release Costa Rica from the corruption and chaos in which the country was drowning: he must throw the rascals out—not just in an election but with bullets and death.

Nearly every weekend we would leave San Salvador and journey out into the countryside. On several occasions we visited a beautiful lake not far from the capital, Lake Ilopango where there were cabins for rent and curving paths for strolling around with cleared spots from which to admire the rolling vistas. Checking back later, it turned out that here my son's existence began.

Sometimes we were invited to visit the large sisal plantations which produced fiber for making rope and bags as did La Lucha. At one visit to the country's most extensive sisal farm, I stepped out of the car to go and greet our host while Pepe, seeing a group of peasants standing at the fence, walked over to greet them. As always he began to shake hands.

"Buenos días. Como están?"

The reaction was the same as with the maids at our first coffee farm. Stupefied silence at the initial greeting, and then slow and groping response, not knowing what to say. But he was undeterred. "Como va la cosecha este año? Es más grande que la nuestra en Costa Rica."

After another hesitation, one of the men spoke.

"Yo no sé nada de Costa Rica. Donde está?" He batted flies away from his face.

"Más al sur. Otro país. Yo soy de allá." Pepe turned and pointed to a large sisal plant near a group of huts where the workers lived. "Porqué es esa mata más grande que las otras?"

Finally, they began to talk and he listened carefully, asking questions and consulting them about the best methods for producing bigger crops. Almost before they were aware of it, they were all farmers together, moving from one row of plants to another, touching the leaves, poking into the earth. Since they faced

115

similar problems, they had a joint interest in helping each other fumble for answers.

Then the host called and Pepe had to leave them. He went around the circle again, shaking hands and saying good-by to each man individually. As he approached his host, he apologized but explained that he liked to talk directly to the peasants working the soil because they were often wise about the particular agricultural conditions with which they had to deal.

For a moment the host looked at him curiously. Then after a brief hesitation, he pointed to the two armed guards on either side of him. The familiar machine guns hung casually in their hands.

"Without my two friends here, nothing in the world would make me go closer than ten meters to my workers over there. They would turn me into chopped meat with their machetes before I could move my little finger." He shook his head. "Everybody tells me that Costa Rica is a strange place and if that's the way you treat your peasants, I believe it."

Chapter X

After more weeks went by, we decided to move on. Pepe had never travelled in Central America so he was intrigued by the prospect of visiting other countries, perhaps to confirm the opinion of his fellow citizens that their country was superior to all others in the area. Their government was more democratic, their educational system more wide spread, their health services covered more of the population. Costa Ricans knew all that, but it was satisfying to go and experience it for oneself. The sweet taste of superiority would help assuage the bitterness of exile.

We flew to Guatemala. Like everyone else traveling in Central America we were surprised by the differences among the five small countries. Though they shared a common language, religion, history, racial mix and ties to Spain, each one was a tiny world unto itself. We left the searing heat and the dull flatness of El Salvador behind and flew over mountains to settle down in the coolness of Guatemala City, the country's capital at an altitude of three thousand feet.

The air was like a cool caress. I felt that I could breathe again for the first time since leaving Costa Rica, and the spectacular landscape was a constant source of delight, the most dramatic in Central America because more broken and oddly shaped. Mountain chains rose on all sides cut by rivers and lakes. Numberless volcanos crowded parts of the countryside, their shapes twisted and unsymmetrical like creations of kindergartners playing with crazy clay.

Three or four days after arriving we hired a car and started out towards Antigua. A big tourist attraction, Antigua was reputed to have 365 churches, one for every day in the year, with monasteries and convents attached to many of the houses of worship. They had preserved relatively complete reports detailing both the social and religious life of the city during the days of the Spanish Conquest in the Sixteenth and Seventeenth Centuries. Since there were tunnels connecting the monks' monasteries with the nuns' convents, it was widely believed that the religious orders behaved like humans everywhere and engaged in considerable to-ing and fro-ing during the passing years. There was even a small cemetery within the grounds of more than one convent where babies were buried. The tiny caskets could still be seen, though rarely did the church authorities discuss their contents.

Three miles beyond the outskirts of Guatemala City the chauffeur stopped the car in front of a small, striped sentry box housing two soldiers. Their uniforms were wrinkled and not too clean, and their feet were bare. Shifting their guns from one arm to the other, they came towards the car.

"Buenos días, Señores. Por favor, los papeles."

We handed over our passports, mine of course in English which they couldn't read. For a minute they held it upside down, then flipped the page over, saw my photograph, and turned the passport around. While one guard examined our papers, the other went towards the back of the car, dragging his gun so that the rifle butt banged along the road.

"Por favor, Señores, bájense."

We got out of the car and the guard began a slow search of the back seat. He looked into a paper bag with a pineapple and some mangos, moved our jackets, turned over a newspaper, pushed aside a collection of maps. He never glanced at us once, never betrayed any awareness of our existence. If he were surprised, or even interested in anything he found, he showed nothing, his impassive face, eyes half closed, immobile and silent. He not only seemed resigned to his fate but also to neither want nor expect any change, today nor tomorrow nor tomorrow.

The chauffeur opened the trunk. The first guard poked around, lifting our suitcase and shoving the jack and spare tire over to one side. The two guards then joined the chauffeur and the three of them stood together chatting a minute. All

118

were Indians, hardly taller than I, square and strong looking, their brown, opaque faces never seeming to smile or to change expression in any way.

"What are they looking for?" I asked Pepe.

"Guns. This is a dictatorship, very repressive. They shoot people down on the street, and they've stationed soldiers on almost every corner."

"What surprises me most about all the ones I've seen is how Oriental-looking they are. If I didn't hear them speaking Spanish, I would be sure they were Chinese or Koreans."

"Well, if you believe the theory that Latin America was populated by people who came across the Bering Straits, then they are Orientals. I wish we had more of them—Orientals, not necessarily Indians. So far as I can see, the Indians live outside the economy: they produce nothing and they consume nothing. Too poor, too uneducated and probably too undernourished to do much except try to exist. They have no contact with any of the institutions of society, not the hospitals, or banks, or government agencies, or schools—nothing. And not only are most of them illiterate, I understand nearly three quarters of them don't even speak Spanish. Just their own Indian languages, such as Quechua."

The guards saluted without looking at us, waved us forward and we rode on. Ten miles down the road, the driver slowed again, stopped at another striped sentry post and other soldiers stepped out. Impenetrable, blank faces, papers shown, trunk opened, car searched. Ride on. During the next hundred miles we stopped at least a dozen more times to go through the same procedure. We learned later that on every highway throughout Guatemala the same routine was followed, every hour of every day.

"How much does all this cost?" I asked.

"Enough to educate every Indian in the country," Pepe answered. "If the dictatorship here didn't squander its resources on such stupidity, they could bring

Guatemala into the Twentieth Century within a few years. If they keep on like this, it will take another eight decades."

Returning to the capital after our visit to Antigua, we were invited to visit a coffee farm near Chichicastenango. I loved the Indian names. They sounded so overwhelming the first time you heard them, but if you approached the multi-syllables firmly and got a running start, they could be conquered and then would flow trippingly off the tongue. Since Spanish is phonetic, each letter is always pronounced the same way no matter what it's combined with, so that the speaker does not confront the baffling mysteries of English pronunciation in which the same combination of letters, such as O U G H, can be pronounced five different ways.

As we approached the coffee farm we saw a young Indian woman walking down the road. She was dressed in the brilliantly colored skirt down to her bare feet which most Indians wore, and her hair was braided in a single heavy strand hanging to her waist. But to our surprise, the hair was golden blond and when she turned towards us, the eyes startlingly blue.

The driver slowed to a stop and said something to her in Quetchua. She answered with no hesitation and from her gestures seemed to be giving directions. A blond, blue-eyed Indian? Where did she come from?

Our destination was in an area like most of the coffee farms in Costa Rica, mountainous and at a relatively high altitude of about four thousand feet. The visit had been arranged by a friend of a friend. We were told that our host's name was Hans Hoffmeier, a wealthy coffee grower whose German family had emigrated to Guatemala before the First World War. Remembering the blond woman on the road, I wondered if she had any connection with our host's relatives or friends.

Hans Hoffmeie's house was made of brown wood, its wide overhanging eaves offering protection from both sun and rain. The porch where we waited for our host managed to seem warm and welcoming, boasting the first rocking chairs I had come across in Latin America. Had they been brought over by his German ancestors to add just the right amount of comfort, their blond wood and cushioned backrests in tiny, flowered fabric keeping alive the memories of the Old Countree?

At the sound of a door opening, we turned. An Indian came towards us, typical dark face, black eyes, Oriental features. Typical and yet—something different. Taller than the others we had seen, clothes like ours and, most surprising of all, actually smiling! Was he the manager, el mandador, of the farm? He approached rapidly, holding out his hand, cordial and gracious.

"Welcome to Guatemala. I understand you have just arrived. I am Hans Hoffmeier."

"You are Don Hans?" We couldn't hide our astonishment.

He laughed. "Everybody reacts the same way. You don't think I look typically German? My mother was from Heidelberg and I went to the university there."

After ordering coffee he began to describe what that area of Guatemala was like. There had been an influx of German immigrants at the turn of the century who had acquired land and started in to raise coffee.

"The Germans make excellent immigrants. They are almost always diligent and frugal, and unlike Americans, they learn to speak Spanish well. Here in Guatemala they married into the families of the local landowners, and began bringing up their own children. After a generation or two they became Guatemalan citizens, like my family."

"Who are the blond Indians I've seen?" asked Pepe.

Don Hans shrugged. "You know how men are. Over the years young Germans would come out without any of their women folk and so they—well, many of the Indian girls are quite beautiful and the inevitable happened."

After a while we were taken around the coffee farm. More or less the same methods of cultivation were used as in Costa Rica though the local coffee was not as fine and did not command as high a price on the world market. The processing plant where the coffee was dried and hulled was familiar, with workers slowly turning the raw beans as they lay spread in long rows on the patio floors. But a completely different method of payment to the peons was used.

As the day ended, the peasants lined up near the door of the processing plant. Don Hans took up a large tin measuring bowl, filled it with black beans and started down the line. Each man cupped his hands and the owner put ten cents into the hands, as many black beans as he could pile in and on top of the heap, a hot red pepper. Its brilliant scarlet hue looked like a ruby against the background of the dark beans. These were the wages for a six hour day of labor.

At dinner that night I looked around the table. Crystal wine glasses, delicious food, a hand embroidered tablecloth down to the floor, mahogany furniture, solid and heavy, silent servants to wait on us. We were surrounded by all the appurtenances of the landowning class in a developing country.

"Why are the roads in Guatemala so primitive?" Pepe asked.

"Because we don't really need them to be any better," Don Hans answered. "We can get an Indian to carry a hundred pounds of coffee on his back nearly a hundred miles and only pay him ten cents. He doesn't need a well surfaced road. Why should we tax ourselves to get something we can live without?"

As the weeks passed and we traveled more and more about the country I slowly became familiar with many of the green valleys which drowsed along the river banks. Wherever we went the villages were resplendent with the colors of the Indians' hand-woven materials. Not just the fabrics but everything about the country seemed to be more intense, the dramatic landscape, the volcanos, history, even the food. I found it was more satisfying than in Costa Rica because more spices were added; garlic, coriander and oregano seasoned most meats and salads. In addition lots of chile was used and the black beans, served at every meal including breakfast, were succulent and luscious. I was grateful to escape for a while (how long would it be?) the tiring blandness of so much of Costa Rica's cuisine.

One of the more shameful chapters in American relations with Latin America occurred in the Guatemala of that time, the 1940's. Skewered by our obsession with Communism, the State Department either permitted the CIA or else encouraged the organization to finance and carry out a coup again Jacobo Arbenz. He had been legally elected in a country which was trying to battle its way out of the shackles of a repressive dictatorship. And his was a country which was also one of our allies. But because its newly elected president was too liberal for the United States, Washington decided that he had to go. And go he did, in a blaze of bullets which were supplied by the CIA to the Guatemalan military, many of whose soldiers and officers were advised by the Central Intelligence Agency. The explanation given was that Guatemala posed a threat to the vital interests of the United States. Guatemala at that time had a population of fewer than five million people.

Chapter XI

Some weeks later we left for Mexico City. Unlike the classic case of people in exile starving in a garret or selling tortillas on street corners, we lived a comfortable, middle-class life. We rented a small apartment in the home of a Costa Rican woman who had settled several years before in a pleasant part of town, Las Lomas de Chapultepec. With her help we set up modified housekeeping, taking our meals with her. Then we bought an automobile and during almost all weekends made trips out into the country exploring in all directions. Pepe opened an office in the center of town and began to buy Mexican ceramics. On the surface we were typical, law abiding, business people who were just trying to get along and live as unobtrusively as possible.

After a short time Pepe's office on Avenida Lopez became the center for many of the Costa Ricans traveling through Mexico. Since more and more of them were opponents of their government, they came to see him instead of visiting either the Consulate or the Embassy. He helped with their business problems and showed them how to negotiate the intricacies of Mexican red tape. If they needed any legal papers, contracts or exit permits to ship goods out of the country, he had his secretary guide them around the mountains of government forms which had to be completed and which made most people break out in a sweat of desperation. In effect he acted as an unofficial consul of Costa Rica and his services were increasingly sought out by friends and acquaintances.

Furthermore, his business office was a perfect cover for what became his obsession, the buying of arms. Though he was committed to the idea of an armed revolution, the Second World War was in full sway, and the acquiring of any kind of armaments was especially difficult; the United States government, abetted by the CIA, did not want a sea of arms washing around Latin America. Too many guns would destabilize an already shaky political situation. Furthermore, the American government was afraid that if it permitted any kind of trading in arms, some would inevitably fall into the hands of the pro-Nazi groups in South America. Those groups were eager to overthrow the few legitimate governments which had managed to survive, and to replace them with German satellites, men dedicated to help with the "final solution of the Jewish problem."

Purchasing arms was the main factor in Pepe's life, but I had a different one. Some weeks before leaving El Salvador I became pregnant. Probably women in that condition are divided into the two famous groups with whom social scientists are so concerned. With a pregnancy the two groups are the lucky ones who welcome their state, and the unfortunate ones who don't. I belonged to the latter group. The idea of having a child frightened me to death. I had no idea how to care for one, what to feed it, or how to handle illness or any other complication. Besides, I disliked small children and even more the slavery which a helpless child imposed on its caretaker. The twenty-four-hour-a-day dedication demanded by a little one had always seemed to me intolerable.

But Pepe, the most undomesticated of men, was happy.

"There is a saying in Spanish that a man has to do three things in his life: plant a tree, write a book and have a son. I have already planted many trees in La Lucha. Now I am about to do the third one on the list. The book will have to wait."

Characteristically, he assumed that the child would be a boy, and that I was as content as he with the prospective heir. He never asked how I felt about the child, and of course I didn't express any of my concerns to him. For a woman not to want children would have seemed to him unnatural to the point of immorality.

"Where do you think the baby ought to be born? If I'm an American and you're Costa Rican, having him here in Mexico seems kind of dumb. But will the government let me go back?"

"He will have to be born in Costa Rica."

Since Pepe saw everything through a political prism, I often wondered what his attitude was towards his child's birthplace. How much importance did he give to the fact that he would become a father while exiled from his own country? Would that have an emotional appeal to his fellow citizens? Would that appeal translate into contributions for the buying of arms? Perhaps he did not know himself how much it mattered to him, his child's country of origin. "Since you're not a Tica, I don't believe the government will object to your returning to San José. We can find out tomorrow at the embassy."

A week later the embassy informed us that the Costa Rican government would not object to my returning to San José

As the weeks passed, our lives ran along a double track. During most of the hours of the day we were the soul of respectability: the careful businessman interested only in Mexican ceramics, his pregnant wife seemingly not involved in anything outside the home, and a few quiet friends coming and going without noise or fuss, polite and colorless enough to fade into the background. Who could suspect that the businessman spent as many hours a day as he could setting up a network of contacts through whom he tracked the arms dealers. Soon he knew exactly who had what at what price and where, when delivery could be expected, where the arms could be stored once purchased, and most important of all, how they could be shipped out of the country without either the Mexican authorities or the CIA suspecting anything.

As time passed, one by one those problems were resolved. It turned out that dealers in guns and ammunition were remarkably numerous, not as many as nowadays, but numbering in the scores. Prices were high or low depending on how many were needed and how soon: if the purchaser wanted them right away, the price went up. After paying what was agreed on, the arms could be hidden in warehouses until the hour when they were loaded into trucks and started on their way to ships bound for Port Limón in Costa Rica. Pepe decided that the safest way would be to smuggle them out of the country hidden in crates full of Mexican ceramics which would be sold in the markets in Central America. As the weeks passed I became aware that the crates were gradually being filled with enough dishes to supply the households of every man, woman and child throughout the Isthmus of Central America.

When Pepe and I were discussing it once, he said casually, "Now that I know how it works, all I have to do is raise the money."

"Why do you have to do it?"

"Because no one else will."

I remembered a conversation we had had long ago in what now seemed another lifetime. He had not yet made the speech which had ended with his being imprisoned, not yet even become more than peripherally involved in politics. He had looked up from a book he had been reading and had said quite casually, "I'll be ready when they need me."

"Who? When who needs you?"

"The country. Sooner or later they will turn to me."

There it was again, that note of fate. There it was again, the absolute certainty that he would be singled out and that national power would be placed in his hands. To anyone who didn't know him, he might have left the impression that he was simply going to wait until the moment when the presidential sash would be slipped over his head while he addressed a grateful nation delirious with joy at his accession—something when it came for which he would have worked unremittingly for countless years.

Now back in Mexico, as far as raising money was concerned, we both knew that he was right. No one else had the dedication or the ability to carry through a project so difficult that it would have defeated anyone else in the country. In fact,

127

in the Costa Rica of that time, the idea would never even have occurred to anyone else. Revolution? Shooting people? Where would you get the guns? How would you organize an army? How supply it? How train it? How would you decide which targets to attack? No one else could be expected to have the answers or to be capable of finding them.

Mexico City in the 1940s was a fascinating place. It was not yet the largest city in the world. It did not suffer from suffocating air pollution or grid-lock traffic jams or over population. For those of us in the middle class with enough money and a certain amount of leisure, the city offered a variety of cultural excitement. Its paintings were full of warmth and color, with Diego Rivera reviving murals and other artists creating in a dozen different media. Mexican marimba music had the nostalgic lilt of lost paradises mixed with the wild rhythm of slaves released from bondage. More than anything else, Mexican architecture exhibited a sense of grandeur, their buildings constructed on a monumental scale of design and size. Perhaps most intriguing of all was the sense of history the country conveyed, the entangling of various racial strains, Aztec, Toltecs, Spanish, American, Chinese, mixed bloods of all countries, stretching back across the centuries, each leaving yet another layer on the society's culture.

My middle getting bigger and bigger, I would walk for miles through the city. Around the Zócalo, (the stupendous central square where an Aztec temple had stood at the time of the Spanish Conquest) there was an endlessly intriguing street life: little boticas selling everything imaginable from traguitos mágicos de amor guaranteeing your lover's eternal adoration to second-hand refrigerators; restaurants and food stalls serving dishes from every country in the world; tiny cubbyholes with just a single counter offering statues of El Corazón de Jesús, the Bleeding Heart of Jesus, along with other religious objects assuring everlasting life, eternity for only five pesos.

One of my clearest memories of our stay in Mexico was my constant loneliness. Pepe was always busy, now consumed by his plans about the revolution. While many of his ideas were shared with me, he was not one to involve the womenfolk in his life in any active way. Partly this was to protect everyone around him who might be questioned. Partly he had a justifiable fear that people would be indiscreet and reveal secrets; half the revolutions of Latin America had been betrayed because someone got drunk in the corner cantina and talked too much. And partly because Pepe was a machista and felt that women should not participate too intimately in affairs of government.

So for most of the hours during the day I was left to myself. Though there were thousands of Americans living in Mexico City at that time I didn't have any contact with them and didn't know how to go about establishing connections. Almost all the Latin women we met were wives and mothers, with no interest in anything outside their families. Though they were warm and often funny, I somehow couldn't overcome my shyness enough to make the leap across the language and cultural barriers to be able to form any real friendships.

For many months after my initial arrival in Costa Rica, I was convinced that I had adjusted well to life outside my own society. I learned the language. I accepted different values with equanimity. I tolerated unfamiliar customs with, if not grace, at least silence. But Mexico was different. And more difficult. Because I had almost no contacts there, and not one of a personal nature, almost from the beginning I had suffered from a growing sense of being alien and alone. Perhaps worst of all, incapable of developing the self assurance needed to cross the chasm of differentness the foreigner is surrounded by.

To have discussed my loneliness with Pepe would have been useless. He would have considered it an intolerable weakness which could be cured by either a more dedicated study of Spanish or else by firing the maid and staying at home to do housework. I therefore resorted to what people have done throughout the ages: I made up companions.

These companions went with me everywhere. We carried on interminable conversations, always in English of course, conversations in which I was brilliant and witty and never once had to fumble for the correct form of the imperfect subjunctive. Strangely enough, they were never Southerners, these companions, but rather hoity-toity folk from either the eastern United States or from Europe. And of course by now I can't remember anything we talked about as we wandered around the city.

Most of all I remember my shock at the pervading poverty. My companions and I were appalled at the hopeless faces of women and little children sleeping in doorways on beds of folded newspapers; at beggars who would come up and touch our arms with a kind of desperate insistence, asking for just a few pennies to buy a tortilla; at cripples, twisted and horrible, dragging themselves along, slowly starving, their eyes sinking deeper and deeper into the hollows of their bony faces.

My pregnancy was advancing steadily, and with it my anxiety. Suppose the child were a girl instead of a boy. Would Pepe show resentment or even dislike? Though I read as widely as possible about how to care for a child, nothing seemed to allay my fears about being unable to care for him adequately. Among other terrors, I had a premonition that the child would die before he was five years old—or at least before he was grown up. The fact that the fears were so irrational only made them more entrenched.

The days slid by. Almost every weekend we would go off in the car to explore Mexico, visiting Taxco, Guadalajara, Vera Cruz, the pyramids, Monterrey, other cities. We would drive for four or five hours, sometimes more, often less, browsing around the mountains and valleys, finding out how the country functioned, who was in control, how the peasants lived, or rather managed to exist, where the wealth came from.

One day the newspapers carried an astounding headline: NEW VOLCANO BORN IN PARACUTIN. We decided to try to drive as close as we could so as to watch the stupefying sight: the earth thrusting itself up to form a new mountain and change the topography of a region. It had first been sighted by a peasant who was walking across a field one morning and saw something unusual: what seemed like a puff of dust coming up out of the earth. As he watched, the dust cloud appeared to grow, and then the earth formed a tiny mound which slowly pushed itself up higher and higher. After watching for a few minutes he ran to his village and told the priest, who came out with several other peasants to see for themselves. They in turn went to the local police and the message moved up the chain until it finally reached the governor of the province.

By then the newspapers had sent someone out to investigate and to photograph. We had hardly read the story before the area around the volcano was being overrun with visitors. Pepe was anxious to observe as much as we could so we drove half the night to come as close as possible to the site. My sharpest memory of that experience was the noise. The volcano's presence was announced from miles away by what sounded like a cannonade. Every two or three minutes there would be a roar followed by an explosion as the volcano would shoot a volley of earth, huge rocks, dust, molten lava and scarlet flames up into the air. Then the side of the growing mountain would explode with light and a river of fire would burst forth, the lava slashing its way down leaving a large collar of material up at the top which drew the mountain up higher and higher.

We drove through the village of Paracutín and out on the other side. Then, about half a mile from the volcano, we parked the car near a small, rickety stable and hired horses for the ride out to the site. The police had encircled the area with ropes and wooden stakes driven into the ground, but many people had simply crawled under the rope and were walking around the stubble at the base. I watched one man take out a cigarette, lean over and light it from a fiery coal. Most of the spectators seemed either unaware and unafraid of the imminent danger, and even the heat radiating from the huge rocks strewn about didn't deter them from approaching within a few feet of the glowing debris. Fascinated and seduced by the unpredictable power of nature, they couldn't resist the urge to close in on the cataclysmic changes pulsing under their feet.

* * * * * * * *

Since it was impossible to gauge the coming birth accurately, Pepe and I decided that it was time for me to go back to San José. He was insistent that the child must be born in Costa Rica, and that it might be dangerous to wait any longer. He arranged for me to go to the house of his sister, Luisita, where I stayed until after the baby was born. And stayed. And stayed. For three whole months. Later, thinking back on it, I often wondered how she had the patience to put up with me and a new born baby, but at the time, she was so gracious and hospitable, she made me feel that my presence was never a burden.

The baby was born on April 20, the birthday of Adolph Hitler. When the nurse put him into my arms, I was stunned.

She's made a mistake! This cannot possibly be my child! He was the first new-born I had ever seen and the shock made me ask myself if all the months of discomfort and hours of pain had been worthwhile. To get this? I had pictured him like the magazine advertisements of eight-months-old babies, fat and rosy and blue-eyed, and above all, smiling. Instead, he was dark, and to my inexperienced glance, seemed to have a slightly purple tinge. I stared down at the black hair and colorless eyes which looked brown when they were open, and I kept wondering how he could have dark eyes when his father and I both had blue-green ones? Baffled and disappointed, I spent hours watching the microscopic face that never smiled but rather seemed to cry all the time.

But more than anything else, I was overwhelmed that he was so tiny! I appealed to my sister-in-law.

"He only weighs seven and a half pounds!"

"But that's a big baby. What did you expect? Ten kilos?" That's exactly what I had expected, twenty pounds more of hearty meat and muscle. How could I ever learn to care for anything so fragile? That first day of his life I was convinced that my fears about his early demise would come true. No one that defenseless could possibly last through the night. And for weeks and weeks afterwards, I was haunted by the same dread that I would wake in the morning to discover that he had died during the hours of darkness.

As soon as Pepe had learned that I was pregnant, he decided that if the baby were a boy he should be named José Martí after the leader of the Cuban revolution against Spain in 1898. So the little tiny thing was given a big name, José Martí, which I shortened to Martí and which over the years has become a favorite name in Costa Rica. To my surprise my Martí didn't die after three days, his eyes began to turn green, and to everyone's relief, he finally stopped crying. With limitless patience Luisita taught me to care for him. I slowly outgrew my fears that he would break in half or that one of his legs would drop off, and in a few weeks I even decided that out of all the world, he was the baby I wanted most of all.

And then it was time to return to Mexico.

Everyone who has ever traveled with an infant is probably appalled at the amount of equipment necessary to maintain the health and cleanliness of a microscopic bit of humanity which only weighs ten or twelve pounds. Pepe's response to his son was probably typical for a Latin American father: he maintained diplomatic relations but did not believe in any entangling alliances. He would pat the baby or cover him if the blanket had slipped off or come and tell me or the maid if Martí were crying. But the idea of picking him up or giving him

133

a bottle was something he felt incapable of doing. The machista mystic took over. Real men didn't play the paternal role to that extent. Once when I remonstrated with him for not having more physical contact with the baby, he enunciated a domestic policy from which he never deviated.

"I will fill the house with maids from the front door to the back, but I will never change any child's pants!" And he never did.

I had been away nearly four months. Since we now had a new member of the family we decided to move into a house, complete with garden and Indian maid. María had the same closed-in quality as the soldiers and maids we had encountered in both El Salvador and Guatemala, the same kind of opaqueness which did not permit any intimacy from outsiders—and she considered both Pepe and me to be light years away from her world.

She was in her fifties, a square, heavy-set woman, hair drawn into a thick braid down her back, wide, brown face devoid of expression, a perpetually impassive mask, silent and indifferent. The day she arrived, sent by a Mexican friend, she set the pattern of our relationship which did not deviate through all the months we knew each other.

Moving silently, she came into the house. I motioned her to a chair so that we could have a chat about what was expected of her. Her face turned slightly aside, she shook her head and remained standing, waiting for me to issue instructions. I was non-plussed for I had expected us to try to establish the beginnings of a friendship—or at least, some tenuous ties.

I first asked if she had ever worked for foreigners before?

Looking down at the floor, she answered softly, using two of the few words with which she was to communicate with me from now on.

"No, Señora."

"Ud podría hacer viajes cortos con nosotros los fines de semana?" I wanted to know if she could travel with us on short weekend trips.

"Lo que la Señora diga." Whatever the Señora says.

The lowered eyes could not be pried above the tile floor, the flat voice remained without inflection. During all the time she spent with us, I was never able to discern if she disliked me, felt at ease, wanted to leave, wished us all dead. Though she was willing to do anything about the house she remained impervious to my efforts to establish contact on any basis more profound than please-clean-the-kitchen or it-is-now-time-to-change-the-water-in-the-flower-vases. No matter what I said to her, the response hardly varied. Whichever monosyllable was required, si or no, always accompanied by Señora, came in a soft murmur, face averted, eyes downcast. But no spontaneity ever greeted me. There was never a hint of impulsiveness, not one single burst of lightness to alleviate the gloom which she seemed to bring into the house even on the brightest day.

* * * * * * * *

During the months I had been gone, Pepe's efforts to collect money for the purchase of arms had progressed. Every cent which came in was immediately funneled into the acquiring of guns and ammunition, which were stashed in warehouses under boxes of ceramics waiting for shipment to Costa Rica. In addition, money had to be collected for bribes to buy Mexican officials, because no arms could be sent out without permits from the Ministry of the Interior. And the constant danger of someone's betraying the whole operation to the CIA was a factor which had to be considered at every encounter.

The weeks melted away. My Spanish was becoming quite fluent, helped along by the months I had spent with Luisita and her family. Now that I was no longer pregnant, I enjoyed Mexico City more. Martí was doing well, Pepe was increasingly successful in raising money and though we were not sure, we sensed that our months in Mexico were drawing to a close. A new government would shortly be elected in Costa Rica and we hoped that we would be permitted to return.

During all the months that we had been out of the country, Pepe had never once mentioned homesickness or regret at being away or anger at not having the right to go back. In fact, except in strict political terms, he had never mentioned the country at all and even less the fact of our exile. But I often had the feeling that the only way he could bear being away from his beloved Lucha Sin Fin was never to let himself bring up the subject. Seemingly, it was too painful to talk about.

The last shipment of arms was finally ready. Packed in with the ceramics, it was nailed into wooden cases marked POTTERY and awaited only the final papers to start on its way to Costa Rica. The Minister of the Interior had instructed us to come to his office at nine o'clock one evening to receive the last permits for the shipment. We told ourselves that by this time tomorrow night, we would have accomplished everything, that all the talking and pleading and convincing would be over. The endless hours of tracking down arms dealers, negotiating, checking on the "merchandise", keeping it all hidden were now about to end. Everybody in the chain of command had been bribed. We had paid off, sworn to secrecy, or subtly threatened every person who had had any connection with the project. Now we had nothing to do but collect the last three or four forms, and check to see that everything had been signed and sealed.

We arrived at the Ministry fifteen minutes before nine. Since Mexicans have a different concept of time and never really believe that anyone will be punctual for any function other than the bull fights, we had expected to wait for an hour at least. Instead, we were hardly seated in an ornate, marble-floored room before an official of the Ministry came to us.

He leaned over and spoke softly.

"Señor, the Señor Ministro will see you now."

It always surprised me how mild Mexican voices were. Even when people were angry they rarely seemed to shout, and the boisterousness of the Cubans or the Puerto Ricans was largely unknown. As we rose to go into the Minister's inner office, we looked at each other, wondering what his immediate acceptance of us indicated. Good news? Bad news?

The official turned to me and his voice seemed even more gentle.

"Talvez la Señora prefiera quedarse aquí."

Though the last thing the señora wanted was to stay here, I stayed, and Pepe went in alone. I stared around at the ornate office, its brilliantly colored rugs, all gold and scarlet and cobalt blue seemingly lit with an inner glow. For some reason the ponderous, Colonial furniture and red velvet drapes drawn back across windows going up twelve feet reminded me of the shivering women and children sleeping on newspapers in the doorways of office buildings. I wondered how much the Señor Ministro was paid a month.

As I waited, I tried not to drum my fingernails on the arms of the chair, or cross and uncross my legs a dozen times or do any of the other annoying things I did when I was nervous. Instead, I leafed through a magazine on the heavily carved table in front of the sofa where the Minister's assistant had seated me. The entire magazine dealt with the Mexican oil industry. It was difficult for me to read because the words seemed to squiggle around on the page and all the photographs of oil rigs and men climbing up on scaffolding swayed back and forth as I tried to concentrate. My hands were so wet and clammy that when I put the magazine down, my fingers were smudged with black from the printer's ink.

The door to the minister's office opened suddenly and Pepe appeared. For a second he stood there without moving, his face blank and expressionless. Then he came forward but didn't stop at my chair and apparently didn't even see me for he continued straight on to the exit door which swung silently open. I followed him down a broad flight of stairs, our heels clacking on each marble step, on to the outside and into the car, still without speaking. The traffic light at the corner flashed red but the car didn't slow down.

"Stop!" I commanded, sure he hadn't even seen the signal.

We jerked to a halt as the eerie silence went on. I looked out at the throngs of people clogging the streets, and for a few seconds my mind shied away to a mystery about Mexicans: when did they sleep? Since most of them worked during the day and didn't seem to start dinner until ten o'clock at night, afterwards often at midnight going to movies, theaters, nightclubs, gambling joints or visits to friends, I decided they must have developed another method for regenerating themselves. Perhaps they used a secret ritual inherited from their Aztec ancestors. Or maybe -

"He demanded another twenty-five thousand dollars."

Pepe's words seemed to ricochet around the car and to keep bouncing back and forth like balls in a pinball machine.

"Twenty-five—but you paid him off months ago!"

"He was quite open about it. He explained that he was only in office for six years and in that time he had to make enough money to take care of his family for the rest of his life."

We drove on, jumping a red light and narrowly missing a truck which had the right of way and had expected us to stop. I could feel my heart pounding in my chest. Pepe's driving was always somewhat erratic for subconsciously he expected everyone to get out of his way, and he was genuinely surprised when the other people on the road assumed that he would obey the traffic rules instead of doing

138

exactly as he pleased. Looking ahead I saw that we were approaching a large intersection with streets feeding in from six different directions.

"Slow down! You're going to get us killed!" The car lost speed and slid to a stop. "What else did he say?"

"He said the money had to be there on his desk by midnight. Or else all the arms would be confiscated."

"But they've been paid for already!"

"This is Mexico. They'll take everything. To raise that much money in two hours—or two months—would be impossible! We've lost it all."

We drove on. As so often happened when faced by an emotional situation, I felt a block of ice congealing around me, walling me off from my surroundings. I wanted to tell him to give vent to his bitter disappointment, to try to let go by cursing or screaming, to rage or yell, but no words would come. Instead, the car seemed filled with his aching silence. Faced by that impenetrable self control I could think of nothing but platitudes which would have sounded almost insulting.

The drive out to Las Lomas de Chapultepec was endless but eventually we reached home. He went around the house mechanically locking doors and windows as he did every night, turning out lights, putting papers and letters in a folder. Once upstairs, though, he sat down on the bed and suddenly everything seemed to stop. Unmoving, he stared at the wall, eyes fixed and unblinking, hands still in his lap. I couldn't even tell if he were breathing. The silence in the room hung like a sound-proof fog which absorbed all noise and left the faint toot of horns from the street sounding phantom-like and remote.

"Pepe, my God, what can we do?"

Immobile and silent, he didn't answer. I could hear a clock ticking in the hall and then the scream of a cat so eerie and far away the high-pitched sound could have come from outer space. I decided he wasn't listening. He had a trick of not answering questions he didn't want to bother with, and just as I was beginning to wonder if that were happening now, he stood up.

"Do? I will tell you what I am going to do. I am going to start again tomorrow morning to raise more money and buy more arms. And right now I am going to sleep."

The next day he started in again. It was a process made more difficult and more lengthy by the failure just sustained. Prospective contributors naturally wondered whether everything would be lost again. But even so, money began to come in. The endless round of talks went on, the repetition of the arguments, the pounding away at objections, the insistence that an armed revolution was the only way. Listening to him going over and over the same speeches, I could never understand where Pepe got his enthusiasm. Every time he had to discuss the matter with anyone, it would require about two sentences and then he would be off: the diamond-hard certainty which rolled over all opposition leaving a group of people who were convinced that he was right. And who were willing to contribute. Again. And again.

We had been in exile for over two years. To Americans the concept of exile is so startling, so bizarre, most of us can only dimly grasp the meaning of it, or of how devastating it can be. Cut off from all roots and often even from all contact with people they know, the exiles face ruin. In order to stay alive they are often reduced to taking menial jobs such as janitors or street cleaners—when those are available. For in many countries where exiles are sent, the local laws prohibit foreigners from working, so unless they find illegal employment, they begin a hand-to-mouth existence which often wrecks their health and their family life.

Fortunately, none of these problems affected us. We had an income from Costa Rica, we had Pepe's brother, Antonio, running La Lucha and the various businesses of sisal, coffee and country stores, and we had generous friends who would have supported us if the necessity had arisen. But even so, we faced the

140

frustrations and consuming rage which people deprived of their country always feel. During the two years we lived in exile, Pepe never once mentioned anything about La Lucha. I was unable to decide whether his silence indicated that his hurt was too deep to talk about or because his rage at what had been done to him was so consuming he was afraid to express anything for fear he might explode into a course of action which would be self-destructive and dangerous.

A new government was about to be elected. Calderón Guardia had picked a henchman, Teodoro Picado, a man who was limited though less destructive, and all reports indicated that he would win the rigged election. We hoped that after the inauguration, we would be permitted to go back to San José. So the days and weeks dragged themselves by while we waited to hear.

One day there was a phone call from Antonio.

"It's turned out the way we expected. Picado has won. How would you like to come home?"

My mind played a strange trick. The granting of anything so long desired often struck with so hard a blow that I could only sit immobile, too stunned to respond. But not Pepe. For once he reacted spontaneously. He whirled around, snatched up Martí and swung him up and down.

"We're going home!" he bellowed. "Home! home! home!" His voice rising to a roaring crescendo, he swung Martí higher and higher.

Terrified, the child let out a shriek, and began to kick frantically to escape. Two friends who were visiting joined in with accompanying roars, pounding each other on the back and letting out a high-pitched ai-ai-ai! which went on and on.

Finally one of them stopped long enough to express what the three men felt.

"Those sons of bitches! They may have won this election but that'll be the last one for a long time!"

He was right: it was many years.

Drawn by the noise, the Indian maid appeared. For a moment she listened to Martí's screams and then silently took him away to a quiet spot outside the house to escape from people whose behavior she regarded as incomprehensible. She did not know where Costa Rica was, did not care and in fact had never even heard of the country, a place which interested her about as much as did the island of Madagascar. She only knew that we paid her regularly and treated her kindly so whatever else we did was of total indifference.

We began to plan that afternoon. There were innumerable decisions to make: what to do about Pepe's office in downtown Mexico City, where to leave the office furniture, typewriters and supplies, when to sell the car, what to do with the furniture in our house in Las Lomas de Chapultepec, how to help our Indian maid find a job with another family. And above all, the same insoluble mystery which everyone who moves faces: how did we acquire such staggering amounts of junk? It is of course always the fault of the other spouse. If he weren't so irrational, if he would just sometimes behave with a teeny-weeny modicum of reasonableness, we wouldn't have these mountains of useless thingies to pack. Why does anyone want to keep ....

But eventually it was all done. We were packed, we had disposed of everything, and with considerable regret we had said good-by to everyone. It was especially painful to part with those few men who had been with Pepe from the early days after our arrival in Mexico City, trusted friends who listened, provided help, came up with practical ideas to solve problems and above all, who didn't talk.

As I look back over my life I seem to see an endless series of partings, from city to city, from country to country and even continent to continent. In spite of my loneliness, I was full of pain at this leave-taking from Mexico City because as so often happens, I had finally found a friend just as we were leaving. She was the wife of an American businessman, a woman who not only spoke fluent Spanish but who had a gift for friendship and who realized its value. As she and I said good-by in our nearly empty living room I had a presentiment that we would never meet again. And we never did. We tried to keep our friendship going with letters which gradually turned into post cards and finally into mere Christmas greetings. Then came the news that she had been killed in an airline accident, just as I was planning a journey which would take me through Mexico City to see her again.

When Pepe and I returned to San José we received a tumultuous welcome. My aunt and uncle had planned a big fiesta and held a kind of open house so that people poured into the garden, the living rooms, the dining room and overflowed into the wide hall down the center of the rooms. There were photographers with popping light bulbs, there were fireworks rocketing across the fence lining the property, there were mountains of food, and microphones into which Pepe and everybody who wanted to made speeches, and there were even a few far-sighted guests who brought their own bottle because they knew that my relatives did not drink alcohol and the idea of a fiesta without liquor was too contradictory a concept to cope with.

It was at this fiesta that I heard for the first time the shout, Viva Pepe! It was to follow him for the next forty years. It was woven through all his political campaigns, it enlivened his every speech, interrupted every meeting, accompanied every public appearance. Viva Pepe! and during the time of the Junta, the cry was often followed by his song, an irresistible, catchy melody written by two musicians to rally the troops up in the mountains. When the vivas and the music had finally stopped, Pepe made a brief speech thanking people for their welcome and indicating that the struggle ahead was going to demand all their strength and dedication.

I was surprised at how well he spoke, for he had had little practice. Speaking before an audience to express political ideas required a technique which usually cost years of effort. But as with so much else in his life, he had a natural talent, and by his obsessive concentration quickly mastered the art. On this first occasion

143

he was wise enough to follow the classic rules for public speaking: stand up, speak up and shut up. He was brief enough not to tire people but took sufficient time to cover the political landscape with precision and insight. And then rounded it off with an emotional appeal to action.

The applause was deafening. I wasn't wise enough at the time to realize that I was present at the first speech in a political career which was to cover forty years and be as brilliant as any in Latin America's Twentieth Century.

Until the end of his life he believed on that day destiny had finally caught up with him.

Chapter XII

Revolutions in a small country are different from vast social movements in large societies. The intimate size of the canvas affects everything, making each decision personal, often painful and usually fraught with immediate impact. In the Costa Rican upheaval, Pepe and I knew most of our fighting men: those of our generation as friends, those who were younger as the sons or brothers of old acquaintances. Many had been at school with Pepe and several were even relatives. The close relationships made for a tightly knit little community, with all the advantages and disadvantages which that kind of situation carried with it.

The fighting began with startling suddenness. For several weeks during February small groups of men started arriving at La Lucha. They came in response to what most of them considered the final straw on the part of the corrupt government. When the opposition candidate, Otilio Ulate, won the presidential election, the Calderón clique had the election annulled and declared that their candidate had triumphed. That provided the spark which set the country aflame.

All day long the future soldiers arrived. They came on foot and in cars, by truck and by bus, a few country fellows even on horseback. If they were of Pepe's generation they were given beds down in the warehouses. If they were young enough to bear it, they were offered piles of dried sisal fiber as a bed and a spot on the cement floor. A kitchen was set up, huge quantities of food began to appear, and during some of my walks with the kids I observed men with rifles moving through what looked like primitive kinds of military drill. Pepe would disappear early in the morning to meet with a growing number of volunteers to organize where and how the future soldiers were to be taken care of.

During his few hours in the house he was increasingly monosyllabic, a kind of passionate intensity about him as though all of his energy were concentrated on the enterprise at hand. One day at breakfast he broke a long silence.

"It's coming closer and closer," he said suddenly.

I watched his face, aware that the blue eyes had a special brilliance. "Shooting? They're going to start fighting?"

"We've gotten word that the government knows something is going on. They are sending a jeep with the Army Chief out to investigate. It will be a dramatic way to begin!"

As he talked he slipped a forty-five pistol into his belt and I realized that for some weeks now he had always gone armed even inside the farm. "I wont be back for lunch. And probably not for dinner. We're trying to train everybody who comes. Most of them don't even know how to shoot, much less anything else. Talk, yes. Shoot, no."

"Have all those crates been opened?"

"Yes. So far, there's enough for everybody. But by this time next week we'll have to have more guns."

His quick footsteps were hurrying him towards the door as he spoke and in another moment he was gone.

The rumors about the government's sending a jeep with the Army Chief of Staff turned out to be true. Accompanied by other officers he was ambushed and killed, the first casualties of the revolution. After that, everything seemed to happen at once. The government moved swiftly to retaliate. It began sending its forces along the Pan American Highway, slowly and warily approaching La Lucha with the plan to surround the farm and to destroy it. When word came from peasants acting as our eyes and ears that government soldiers were advancing, Pepe realized that La Lucha and his army's headquarters down in a narrow valley

146

could not be defended. Overnight he decided to move out. Everything was loaded onto trucks, horses, into oxcarts. All members of the Revolutionary Army started across the mountains to a little town, Santa Maria de Dota, to settle down and await reinforcements.

He left without letting me know or saying good-by. It was one in a long chain of actions which hurt me deeply and which I never understood. Did he not trust me enough to keep quiet? Did he not want me to know anything so if I were caught I could not reveal his whereabouts? Or did he simply behave like a Nineteenth Century man who felt that he could make any decision he wanted to and it had to be accepted? In this and in many other situations he never explained anything and refused to discuss his behavior. On this occasion I simply woke up the next morning to find him and all traces of the army gone—for a little while I didn't even know where.

It turned out that my two children and I had been left in the care of my brother-in-law, Cornelio, who was managing La Lucha at the time. The plan was for his wife and children, along with us, to remain at the farm a little longer and then go in a different direction from the army, back into the mountains where we would presumably be safe. But none of this was explained to me. I wasn't even given instructions about what safety measures I was to take to protect our children.

Trying to recover from the shock of the army's having moved out, I sat with a book in my hands towards the end of the day. Without warning, the Revolution invaded the house like a rattle of gunfire. Cornelio Orlich rammed the door open, his breath coming in a short burst.

"Get packed! We're leaving in fifteen minutes! Just bring something warm for the kids, blankets, any fresh food you have. We've got rice and beans. Bring a flash light. Hurry! It's nearly dark already." The sound of his rapid footsteps retreating down the grave path covered all other noise.

I dragged two blankets from the beds and spread them on the floor: Extra shoes for the kids, small wrinkled underpants in case of an accident, sweaters and a change of clothes. Racing to the refrigerator, I wrapped a tomato, some carrots and three bananas in newspapers, dropped them into a bag, tied the ends of the blankets together into a large, clumsy knot. Pushing the food on top, I knew it would probably get squashed. For a second there seemed nothing else to do. Dazed and trembling I stood in the middle of the room, realizing that the 1948 Revolution had finally come home.

I learned that when you were escaping, it was not so much what you took as what you left behind: the photograph of your mother in her wedding gown in the dented silver frame, the Bible you were given when you memorized the Presbyterian Shorter Catechism, your college Shakespeare with the passages marked in wavering lines of different colored ink, the harmonica you played in front of the fireplace in the family's summer home in the Smokies.

I closed the door softly and started down the path to the river, wondering if I would ever come back.

The wooden oxcart that was to go with us, its solid wheels painted bright orange and covered with multi-colored designs, was already loaded. Cornelio and the oxman were tying down the final pieces of food and clothing. Accompanying us were the oxman's two toddlers and his wife with a newborn baby in her arms, the four of them wedged into the oxcart among the bags of black beans and rice. We shivered a little as the tropical evening came swiftly down and a chill wind promised a cold night. Though only ten degrees north of the Equator, La Lucha's altitude guaranteed that we would be bothered by the cold. After a final tying of knots on the cart, the oxman took his place before the two animals and Cornelio gave the order.

"OK, vámonos. Caminemos hasta que la luna salga." He turned to me. "We'll walk as far as we can before the moon rises." In spite of the fact that my Spanish was now so fluent I had no difficulty in speaking and some nights even dreamed in Spanish, Cornelio liked to practice his English and so always addressed me in my language, though most of the time now I wasn't even aware of which idiom I was using.

The oxman's goad came down across the yoke in a sharp crack. The cart lunged forward, forded the shallow river running through the farm, and the twelve of us started up the steep, winding road on the other side, heading for a safe place farther back in the mountains. Martí was managing all right, holding tightly to my hand and pretending not to be afraid because, after all, he was five. But my daughter stumbled over the ruts and gullies, her three-year-old legs slowing us almost to a halt. Puffs of dust rose from our every step, making progress more difficult. Try as we could, it was impossible for the three of us to keep up and we gradually fell farther and farther behind the dim figures up ahead and the soothing clunk of the oxcart.

Cornelio was suddenly beside me.

"You'll have to carry her. We can't afford to go this slowly." The anxiety in his voice made my heart thud. I picked her up and we moved forward. A thousand times before I had easily carried her around, a fat little girl, nimble and squshable, squealing happily as she climbed over everything. Now she seemed to weigh a hundred pounds. The road got steeper; Martí needed more help as we faced into a cutting wind, and the rutted tracks underfoot had been designed to trip the unwary.

I tried not to look at the horizon and especially tried to make myself believe that the sky was not really slowly, slowly turning lighter. Soon the moon would be up, exposing our escape. Pulling Martí along and fighting for breath I quickened our pace, feeling that my back would break as the sleeping child on my shoulder got heavier and heavier. Miles of trudging followed. We moved up and up, muscles begging to rest, trying not to slow down, forcing myself just to keep on keeping on. I couldn't remember when we had last eaten and then realized that water would have been more welcome than food.

"Mommy, I'm cold!" Martí's voice was a nagging whine which ripped through my nervous system making me want to slap him.

"I know. Me too. But we're almost there."

"Where?"

"Where we're going to spend the night. Then we'll be warm."

"Can I sleep with you?"

"Of course. I'll hold you all night. It's just a little farther." Was it? Was it really?

In spite of weariness and cold, at last I became aware that gradually, imperceptibly, we were beginning to overtake the others, a collection of phantoms plodding silently along as they bent into the wind, seemingly tied by invisible ropes to the lumbering cart.

A shadow at my side turned into Cornelio. "Please, couldn't we stop and rest?" I whispered. "Just for a second?"

"No!" His voice cut across the wind. "Don't you understand? We've got to make it to that little shed on the other side before the moon rises. Otherwise, they'll see us and start shooting." Then he added more gently, "Here, I'll take her."

I handed over the sleeping child. For a tiny space of time I enjoyed exquisite relief, free of the dead weight and able to relax my aching muscles. But she woke up almost at once and feeling someone unfamiliar, let out a howl of fear. Cornelio put his hand over her mouth, shook his head, and gave her back to me.

We kept walking. At an altitude of 8000 feet, you feel that every step is weighed down by a leaden boot. Below and behind us lay La Lucha, the mountains rolling away on every side, to the Atlantic in one direction, to the Pacific in the other. As had happened to me so often during the six years since I had come to Costa Rica, I asked myself once again what was I doing here. Here on a trail stumbling through the mountains about to be shot while my husband hid away in a distant valley at the head of a rag-tag bunch of crazy young revolutionaries, shooting grandfather's old hunting rifles and trying to topple a corrupt regime dominated by crooks and communists. I reflected that I should be safely back in Alabama, going to dances at the country club and training to be a newspaper reporter. And then I remembered why I had been so desperate to leave home: too much orthodox Presbyterianism, too much family pressure to conform, too narrow a horizon over which to spread my wings. If we survived, Costa Rica was where I wanted to be.

The trail made a sudden loop, and just as the moon rose above the horizon, we rounded the last curve and I heard the most beautiful sound in the world: an oxcart no longer going up hill. Our shelter was a twenty-foot hut open on one side where a stripping machine had been set up to scrape sisal leaves clean of their green covering, revealing the fiber from which rope and bags were woven. The traitorous moon, earlier bent on revealing us to the enemy, had switched sides and was now our friend, providing the only light we had for unpacking. We spread blankets on thick piles of dry fiber, and too tired to care about discomfort or even the danger we faced, in minutes we had all slid down into layers of unconsciousness.

* * * * * * * *

Breakfast the next morning was cold rice and black beans, cold because we were afraid to call attention to ourselves by lighting a fire. The food was provided by the oxman's wife. In an agricultural society, country people rarely go anywhere without taking some cooked food. Experience had taught them that travel was uncertain and that bad weather might intervene bringing torrential rains which turned their roads into quagmires. Since the unforeseen almost always occurred, they accepted Murphy's Law as a given.

A friend of the oxman suddenly appeared, bringing us more food and a full load of rumors. The government forces, the Bad Ones, were closing in around La Lucha, the stories ran, and were planning to burn it down to the last stick. They would destroy the rope factory, the store, the peasants' cottages, the warehouses full of fiber and what hurt me the most, our home—along with the books in the oven.

"Y, Señor," the peasant said, addressing Cornelio, "hay otras cosas. Y peores todavía."

So there were worse things.

"How much worse can it be?"

"The Bad Ones sent word to Don Pepe that they are tracking the Señora and when they catch her, they will shoot her and the little ones too—if he does not surrender."

Cornelio lit a cigarette. "And what did Don Pepe answer?"

The peasant hesitated a moment and crossed himself. "He said,—but of course, there was a mistake. He said, Shoot them! I will never surrender! ... But of course, there was a mistake. I am sure he did not say that."

I was sure that he had. Like a good revolucionario, he was obligated by his commitment to the cause to let his followers hear him proclaim his total dedication. But I was also sure he had arranged an ingenious way for us to escape.

In the meantime, we had no recourse now but to hide out during the day and travel only at night. Our little group settled down to wait for the protecting darkness.

In front of our hut was a thick wall of dirt which had been left there as a windbreak. Extending several yards in either direction, the wall provided protection as long as we didn't stray into the open. But that proved easier said than done. Trying to entertain two small children cooped up in a few square yards of bare ground without any toys or games a few lacerated my nervous system and turned me into a shrew whose voice got screechier and more piercing as the day dragged along. I did everything I could think of: told stories, created trucks and boats out of the few sticks we found, scraped dirt off the wall to make mud pies, tried to construct a house from the big and small rocks which turned up.

It was one of the longest days of my life. Looking back on it now I wonder if it would have helped if Fate could have revealed something of my children's future: that my daughter would grow up to become the Minister of Foreign Trade or that my son would be the founder and manager of large enterprises providing work and a better life for hundreds of country people. Perhaps it would have shortened those endless hours of vigil, made funnier the rambling stories I invented to try to keep the children quiet, turned the cars and trucks we constructed into golden coaches fit for a Fairy Godmother. Who knows? My memory is that I aspired only to survive until nightfall when we could escape from our prison under cover of darkness and continue our journey.

During much of that day we had heard sporadic gunfire from the government forces camped across the valley. We supposed that they could see our hut but that their guns were not powerful enough to reach us. We were soon to discover that that was not the case. For a few moments I became absorbed in constructing a truck with our sticks and took my eyes off Martí. Intent on following a lizard, he wandered beyond the limits of our protective barrier, and without warning, the world seemed to explode around us.

A burst of machine gun fire ripped across the wall and the bullets smashed into the field beyond the hut, each shell sending up a puff of dirt, poof, poof, poof, poof, too fast to see or count. Screaming his name, I started after him. He didn't understand what was happening and stood still for what seemed like hours, a perfect target for anybody who cared to shoot. The distance between us appeared to lengthen as I stumbled forward over the rough ground, in my imagination seeing him already covered with blood, and then dying in my arms.

"Martí! Come back!"

He turned at the sound of my voice, confused and uncertain, as the guns opened up again. Frightened, not knowing which way to turn, he half fell as he started first in one direction and then in another, baffled by the noise, wondering what he should do.

"Martí, please don't get killed! Please!"

I tried to hurry, lurching along the rutted road, calling his name over and over. Through my tears I could see nothing except his small face as he concentrated on staying upright while he picked his way among the rocks and hillocks of the dusty trail.

"Come back!"

He was working his way towards me now. But he would stop every now and then to find a firm footing, starting one way, changing his mind, slipping a little as he tried to find a solid path. I watched him move in what seemed agonizingly slow motion, unaware, probably even unafraid of the guns across the valley.

Just as they opened up again, the interminable journey finally ended. Exhausted, I reached him, grabbed his sweater and dragged him back to sink down behind our barricade. Over his shoulder I could see where the bullets had ripped down a line of sisal plants and had torn out a section from each six foot leaf, leaving a ragged hole along the whole row. Because I was so frightened, I was about to give way to a burst of rage when I saw his face, bewildered and terrified, eyes beginning to fill with tears. Instead of the blaze of anger, I snatched him up again and we clung to each other wordlessly, glad to be alive and unscathed.

Throughout the days that followed I was constantly assailed by a feeling of unreality. This could not be happening to me, the endless walks through the mountains, the gunfire in the distance, sleeping in huts along the way, cooking over an open fire. And the rumors were the worst of all. My husband had been killed, or the government was surrendering, or La Lucha had been destroyed, or the American Army defending the Panama Canal was planning to move against us. While the rumors invariably proved false, the constant talk about death and destruction had a shattering effect; I suffered frequent attacks of sleeplessness which robbed me of strength and at times of even the ability to function at all. What would happen to us, with Pepe killed, La Lucha destroyed and the cause for which we were fighting defeated? Death by firing squad had been one of the answers.

During those blacker moments, Cornelio and I discussed what to do. We decided that if the worse came to the worst, we would cut back through the mountains and try to walk to Panama, the country on our southern border.

"How far is it?" I asked.

"Over two hundred kilometers. But that's not the worst part."

"Walking two hundred kilometers with four little kids is not the worst part?"

"No. It's the cold. We'll have to cross a range of mountains going up more than four thousand meters—that's over thirteen thousand feet. It's the only overland route. Without protective clothing, people have frozen to death from the winds and the altitude."

"Well, we'll just have to do it. I'm stronger than Carmen so she can ride in the oxcart with the kids. They can all keep each other warm. And somehow we'll make it."

Brave words. But during my hours of sleeplessness, when waking nightmares were the most devastating, I lived that journey over and over: I would spend the rest of my life carrying my three-year-old daughter and leading Martí, wearing shorts and tennis shoes, through endless mountain passes while we slowly froze in the numbing cold...

Toward evening of the next day, we started out again. It was more of the same, up and up steep roads which crawled along the flanks of mountains or else went right over the top—since oxcarts can inch along very steep trails with no need for banking curves or for making grades less precipitous. We had reached an altitude now where most agriculture had been abandoned and where cleared pasture lands and cattle had largely taken over the landscape. If we hadn't been so worried, we could have drawn comfort from the scenery. The central part of Costa Rica was an endless series of mountains and valleys, blue and green and smiling, darkened in some places by thick coverings of trees, lightened in others with cleared places where farming was carried on. It was infinitely sweet and gentle, with sunsets to break our heart and flowering shrubs and vines growing in every empty spot.

For me, however, there was a much greater comfort than the ravishing views: Muni had now decided she was no longer afraid and would ride in the cart on top of a sack of black beans. Now I had nothing to do but to watch Martí to see that he didn't lag too far behind. He was a dark, solemn child, too serious, too concerned about everything, too prone to feel that anything that went wrong was somehow his fault. And the terrifying scene the day before, with the bullets coming so close, did nothing to ease his burdens. In fact, he told me years later that all during the Revolution he had felt that it was up to him to take care of me.

Several hours of walking later, we reached another stopping place, a milking shed belonging to a peasant farmer. He had done business with La Lucha and was an acquaintance of Cornelio's who, as manager of the farm, had handled the transactions. Graciously and with a ceremonious sweep of his hand the farmer motioned us to the shed and made us welcome. Then his wife and children appeared, helped us spread blankets for our beds, warned us to be careful where

156

we stepped, and disappeared briefly into the house to heat up some rice and beans and to bring us coffee.

My sister-in-law, Carmen, and I sat on a pile of corn husks and waited to be served. Through the open window of the hut I could see the peasant woman scurrying about, banging pots and pans as she fumbled over her wood stove to prepare food for her unexpected guests.

"Maybe we should go and help her with dinner," I suggested to Carmen. "She looks so harassed. And that damn smoke from the stove must be blinding her."

For a moment Carmen stared at me, too startled to speak. "Go into the kitchen? Oh, no. She would hate that. She's never had people like us in her house. She would be embarrassed to have us see how she lives."

I realized then that in spite of everything that was happening, war, revolution, the destruction of property, escaping into the mountains, despite all that, class lines were still going to be preserved. During the weeks we were living in the mountains, I didn't wash a dish, cook a meal or fetch or carry anything. The peasant family traveling with us would not have been at ease seeing two señoras washing dishes for that might have implied that the oxman and his wife weren't being sufficiently solicitous of our comfort.

As we were folding our blankets and starting to pack up the next morning, a peasant appeared. Having grown up in the city, I never got used to the way country people simply materialized in front of me. I never saw them approaching, never watched them coming closer. They were always just suddenly there, a few feet away, unfailingly polite, usually smiling, almost always anxious to please. Accompanying this peasant now was another man, taller and heavier, the quality of his clothes proclaiming that he was a city slicker.

Cornelio turned, saw the stranger, and breaking into a wide smile, began to run towards him. They gave each other great bear hugs with loud poundings on the back, both talking at once, interrupting each other without waiting to hear what the other was saying.

"My God, José Luis!" he shouted. "What are you doing here?"

"I arrived yesterday. Pepe sent me to find you."

"How did you know where to look?"

"All the peasants around here are keeping watch on you. This man brought me straight here."

"That's no great comfort. If they all know then the government troops probably know too."

"I don't think so. Everybody in this whole area is on our side." He smiled while he and Cornelio patted each other. "It's good to be home."

"Did you kill off all your patients in that medical school in New Orleans?"

"Just about. Tulane couldn't wait to get rid of me."

Cornelio turned to me. "This is my kid brother. He's just finished his studies. In no time at all he'll wreck every hospital in the country."

José Luis then explained what Pepe had arranged for us. Carmen and I and the four children would be taken to the camp of the American engineers who were building the Pan American Highway down to the Panamanian border. We would be safe there, protected by my American citizenship.

After a wait of several hours, we heard the sound we had been waiting for. Faint, far away, it was a distant motor coming closer. But was it really ours? Was it the truck to pick us up? Or was it theirs? It was coming closer, getting louder, fading slowly and then becoming more clearly audible depending on the dips and curves of the road. If it were theirs, what could we do? The milking shed offered no protection; it was made of flimsy boards not thick enough even to slow down a bullet, much less stop it. Around us the pastures stretched away on every side, with not a tree in sight.

By now the sound of the motor was a steady groan, an engine grinding along in low gear, pulling and hauling itself up and down the steep grades. I picked Muni up and called Martí, planning to start walking, away, over there, anywhere. Better to be shot in the back trying to escape than be shot in the front because of having made no move. But José Luis' voice stopped me.

"It's ours! I see the green and white flag!"

Around the curve in the road chugged a rattle-trap red truck, bumper shaking, top slightly askew, tires skinned like a carpet too heavily traveled. Two crude flags of green and white stripes flapped proudly, albeit at a slightly drunken angle, from each dented fender.

The driver hopped out, his steel-rimmed glasses sliding down his nose as he accepted a plate of black beans and rice and some strong coffee. He was a young lawyer and part time teacher at the university, and now a revolutionary. In answer to our questions he reported on the progress of the struggle.

"There's been fighting. Not much, but some. And so far we've been able to beat them back. Lots of their poor soldiers are from the coast and are not used to cold weather. They were just given a rifle, a bottle of rum and a blanket, and were sent up here into the mountains. They're so cold they can hardly move, much less fight. Many of them don't even have shoes. But as far as we're concerned, people are joining us every day. "

Cornelio asked, "How's the food holding out?"

"Fine. All the country people for miles around are bringing in carts full of everything."

While he talked the rest of us loaded on our gear. If the womenfolk and the children were sent to a safe place, the men would be free to join Pepe and the other soldiers in the army. Unlike many revolutionary movements whose troops were made up of workers and landless peasants, our "Army "was composed largely of young professionals, architects, lawyers, bankers and doctors who had just had enough of a government rotted with corruption and incompetence. And having been thwarted in bringing about change through the democratic process, they had uncharacteristically sought better government by resorting to arms.

After abrazos all around, the six of us piled into the truck, the two women in front, the four children under a dirty tarpaulin in the flatbed at the back. The gears ground, the rattles rattled and we jerked forward, to begin a journey which for discomfort I still remember. But I didn't mind. It was better than walking, it was better than being lacerated by the wind and it was better than carrying a three-year-old child.

We were bound for a place called Villa Mills. I only knew vaguely where it was, somewhere in the cold mountain passes in an area called the Cerro de la Muerte, the Range of Death. The camp was along the track laid out by the American engineers who were constructing a hard surfaced, all weather highway to run north from Panama, through Central America, Mexico and the United States up into Canada. Its purpose was to move men and supplies to and from the Panama Canal in case of blockades of either American coast during the Second World War.

I can't remember how long the trip to Villa Mills lasted. We arrived late in the afternoon, rattling in through large gates in a fence enclosing a camp which spread over many acres. The engineer in charge of the camp, Hal Thompson, was type cast for the part, tall, slim and laconic, wearing muddy boots and a leather jacket. He was hospitable and kind, though obviously baffled by an American scatter-brained enough to get mixed up in a Latin revolution. It wasn't until later that he expressed what he really felt at seeing me, and none of it was flattering. And even less did it indicate any understanding of how another society functioned.

160

Now as I followed him down the hall to the room where my children and I would be sleeping, I listened to his heavy, booted tread on the bare floor and was reminded of my father. They both had the same slow, long stride, measured and careful, the way an experienced engineer would always walk. Impossible to imagine either man giddy enough to engage in any twistings or turnings along the way; under no circumstances would those prudent footsteps ever succumb to any impulsive dashes or deviations, to sudden dartings hither and thither. Rather, they would calmly advance with all deliberate speed towards a distant goal decided upon often years before.

* * * * * * * *

The camp at Villa Mills consisted of a collection of wooden buildings arranged in military rows. There were barracks, offices, a large mess hall and kitchen, a machine shop and an assortment of sheds and open garages where much of the machinery was kept out of the weather. Huge tractors and earth moving equipment, all painted acid yellow, waited in the sheds, ready to be sent out to cut and carve and push the road through a surprisingly hostile environment. Not because of snow or ice or wild animals or vicious tribesmen shooting poisoned arrows. But the engineers faced an opponent perhaps more destructive than anything they had contended with before.

Rain.

None of the top men had ever worked in mountain terrain at nine thousand feet where it rained six or seven months in the year, sometimes twelve hours a day. With the resulting mud. And the slides. And the washouts. Though the engineers had been warned that the huge earthmoving equipment they had used so successfully in other parts of the world would not work here, they were unconvinced. After all, their machinery was the last word in technology. And

American engineers rightly considered themselves among the best in the profession.

They started working, fortunately in the dry season. The road moved higher and higher, the wonderful yellow giants pushed everything out of the way and progress followed stride by stride. Everyone was rightly pleased that the dire predictions had not come true. The engineers joked among themselves and insisted that all those worriers were little old ladies who didn't understand how powerful their sunshine machines really were.

And then the rains came.

The huge yellow earthmovers began to slow down. At first the American technicians refused to believe that the equipment was failing them. It was the fault of the local tractor drivers who couldn't handle machinery that big. The foreigners watched in silent astonishment as the roadway turned into a twisting morass of mud which got deeper and deeper as the days passed. The rains never seemed to stop. Or the sides of mountains to remain in one place. Soon the heavy machinery was settling down into the deepening mud, and even the tractors brought in to pull out the earthmovers got stuck. So after sufficient cursing and blaming and telegraphing and replanning, the engineers had simply built a camp, Villa Mills, high up in the mountains along the track to Panama, and decided to wait for the dry season to roll around. And that was the camp where we settled down to sit out the revolution.

We stayed there for about a month and a half. Almost all of my memories of that period have faded and I have now only a clear remembrance of waiting. As the hours crawled by I began to have the feeling that I had spent my whole life waiting. Torrential rains would pour down unexpectedly and even if we were undercover, the dampness and cold would creep in everywhere. I was hungry for news about what was happening but was afraid to call Pepe directly for fear the lines were tapped. That meant we had no way of learning anything except by the

162

radio, which was in the room of the head engineer, Thompson. Every morning we would have our American breakfast and he would pass on the developments of the preceding day, but I was never sure how much had been edited out or misinterpreted.

The first morning at breakfast Thompson told me the news of yesterday, about which I knew more than he, and then delivered a lecture.

"Any gringo ought to have better sense than to get mixed up in something like this revolution. Well, I mean, everybody knows these people are unstable and child-like. Just look at 'em. Dictators, crazy generals killing people, starting wars—they're just like a bunch of little kids. Now if they would just listen to us, we could help them set up a good, solid democracy, have a few elections. Then everybody could stop all this messing around, and start building roads everywhere so they could get their products to market and everybody would make a lot of money."

"But democracy is a hard system of government to make work. You need a high level of education, or at least lots of people who're dedicated to making it function," I objected.

"No, you don't. It's not hard. Look at us. We've been doing it for two hundred years. No big deal."

When I started to protest that all the circumstances in the United States were different, he looked at his watch and said he had to go.

My other memory is of the cold. It was so penetrating that when someone gave me a parka, the kind American troops used in Alaska, I wore it day and night for the duration of our stay. Though the camp had its own generating plant, each room was bleakly lit by a single weak bulb hanging down from the center of the ceiling, and no power could be spared for heating. After the sun went down, when the cold would intensify, my children and I would huddle together under the parka, all three of us usually sleeping in the same bed for warmth. Whoever was the coldest got to sleep in the middle until someone else demanded the best place.

About halfway through our stay in Villa Mills, a truck appeared suddenly at the gate. It was the same rattletrap in which we had arrived. The driver, this time a young architect, was bound for Santa Maria and Pepe had asked him to stop by and pick me up. I was excited at the prospect of seeing him for we had been separated for several weeks without even a phone call to bridge a distance I sensed was growing wider as he became more and more involved in the Revolution.

Not long after noon we arrived at Santa Maria, a tiny town which was designed like almost all Latin American villages around a small square. On one side was the church, with the school across from it and a couple of little government buildings ranged close by. Pepe had taken over the wooden, one-story schoolhouse for his Headquarters and the green and white flag waved lazily in front; but there were few other indications of a military presence. The two or three jeeps parked in the rear of the school were hardly menacing and even less so a small group of men with old rifles who stood about laughing and making jokes. Aside from that, the life of the town went on undisturbed—except that there were no classes for the children.

As I came into the building I saw Pepe through an open door a few seconds before he saw me. He was wearing a khaki shirt and trousers, with a matching military cap like those of the American Air Force. A local dressmaker, who of course had never seen anything like it in her life, had designed and created the uniform. The seams wobbled a little and the fit was not exactly perfect, but it all somehow tied in with a society which had traditionally been more at ease with butter than with guns. He looked thinner but in good shape, and as always there seemed to crackle from him a field of magnetism, almost visible rays of energy which filled any room where he happened to be. His intense blue eyes, like small bolts of lightning, flicked from face to face as he talked, and listeners usually felt, the first time they met, that they had been hit by a jolt of electricity.

Before I could speak he looked up and came forward to kiss me. "How are you?" he asked, and then turned away before I could answer. I was irritated by his seeming indifference, for I had looked forward to this meeting after our separation and especially after the dangers we had both faced. Of course, I thought, he's making the world safe for democracy and overthrowing dictators and everything else, but dammit, he could exhibit a little more warmth and tenderness.! But oblivious as always to personal feelings if they did not forward his plans, he waved towards the schoolhouse and invited me into his "office."

There were maps everywhere, a microphone, a radio, wires running to a transmitter, and several sheets of paper covered with his handwriting. It was a speech he would give that same night. It would become famous as the Second Proclamation, a call to arms to the country as a whole and a brief outline of some of the plans for the country's future. We had coffee with a group of officers in our Army of National Liberation. Aside from two men who were Pepe's age, forty-two, all the others were in their late 20's or early 30's. Half of them wore horn-rimmed glasses, a few had books sticking out of their pockets, almost all were either university students or else young professionals. They were busy now planning strategy, coping with problems of supply, and helping to write messages and speeches to be delivered over the radio on every other night.

An hour passed and then a second. I began to realize that Pepe and I were not going to have any time to talk alone. I had to return to Villa Mills right after night-fall because the truck was needed back in Santa Maria to help haul supplies. But no one seemed to notice the passage of time. The conversation spun on and on as new problems were brought up and new solutions proposed and discussed.

After a while I left the schoolhouse and went for a walk. I was hurt and angry that he was so absorbed in his problems that he would take no time off for a private moment with me. I began to wonder if this were the kind of life I really wanted. Was being an appendage who was not permitted to participate in anything outside the home the role which could be satisfying to anyone with more than half a brain? Was is possible for an appendage to ever reach the point of establishing some modicum of independence, enough to grasp the reins in her own hands and become autonomous? Later I was to realize that that afternoon in Santa Maria was the beginning of what was to become a pattern with him: total absorption in plans and projects, with no time at all for any personal life. In fact, years were to pass before I could accept the truth: it is unrealistic to expect that anyone pursuing political power will also be a good spouse, parent or even friend. Each of these occupations requires not only time and energy but above all, a sense of commitment. And the political leader has none of the above for a private life. He is always otherwise engaged.

As I climbed into the truck to start back to Villa Mills, I couldn't help wondering why I had come. Was the real purpose of the trip to glimpse some truth about the future?

Once back at the camp, the waiting started again. We had been there about a month when word came that something was afoot. At Santa María I had heard talk about a possible attack on Cartago, the second most important city after the capital, but final plans had not yet been completed. Whenever a truck came by or any chance traveller, Carmen and I would beg and plead for news and then chew over it for hours afterwards. We were aware that if Cartago could be taken, the way to the capital would probably be open and then the Revolution would have a chance to triumph. The road to victory, however, seemed studded with a multitude of ifs.

I filled in the time in various ways. My children and I took walks, explored the surrounding countryside, played in every available spot around the machine shops, the parked tractors, the earth movers and on anything else which stood still long enough to climb on. Whenever they asked me about the machinery I either answered factually, if possible, or imaginatively, if not. I had three Golden Rules in dealing with children: never explain your decisions, never back down and NEVER feel guilty. To that I now added a fourth: never admit you don't know. Make up, invent, change the subject or switch their attention to something you do know, like Hamlet's Soliloquy or the Preamble to the Constitution.

They had now reached the stage where their command of English was getting firmer and firmer. When they were first learning to talk they would try to speak to me only in Spanish. But I was determined that they must speak English correctly and without an accent, an undertaking which was more burdensome than I could have imagined. At first they would use Spanish for the main words in the sentence. "Mommy, yo voy to the casa of my amigo this noche."

"Sorry. I don't speak Spanish. Say it to me in English."

They would try again. "Mommy, I go to the casa of my friend this noche."

After a certain number of attempts the complete sentence would come out in English, though many times it nearly drove us all crazy. Other times when I saw that the struggle was too much, I would let them get away with spontaneous outbursts in Spanish until they had recovered some semblance of relaxation. But now, most of the time, the language problem had disappeared and English "rolled trippingly off the tongue."

Somehow the time passed. One day I was sitting huddled in my parka when my door opened and my sister-in-law, Carmen, eased into the room. Her fine face had a marked resemblance to Pepe's, the Figueres family genes obvious in both of them. She was full of warmth and tenderness and had a charming way of bursting out laughing at anything that caught her fancy. Now she put her finger to her lips in a dramatic gesture and tiptoed over to my chair. Her voice sank to a conspiratorial whisper.

"We've taken Cartago! The government forces there have surrendered!" I jumped up and we did a wild, silent dance, afraid to express anything openly for fear it might not be true.

Sitting on the bed, we spread the parka over both of us and she answered my questions.

"Who went? How many?"

"Everybody."

"Everybody? All six hundred of them?" She nodded. "How did we get through the enemy lines?"

"We crossed over at the Gamboa's farm, at that pass. Pepe knew that at this time of the year, the Trade Winds blow heavy clouds over that whole place. Everything is hidden. He spread the rumor that the Virgin had helped us by sending a special cloud. They all got through! Oh, Pepe!"

"How did you find out?"

"That lawyer boy, the one who brought us here, came by on his way to San Isidro, down the road there. And he told me."

After the fall of Cartago, the government was willing to start negotiating. It took days and days of talk, partly because Latins were verbose and enjoyed making speeches, and partly because there was a cast of thousands. The Archbishop, Monseñor Sanabria, arrived in a jeep. Dressed in flowing ecclesiastical robes he managed to keep his dignity in spite of a huge flag of the Catholic Church which flapped about his ears and which was designed to protect him in case the shooting started again. He was spotted by Alberto Marten, who lead him to a safe shelter.

"Monseñor, you must not expose yourself. Some of our soldiers are still somewhat exuberant. They might keep on with target practice, using anything that moves."

The communist leader, Manuel Mora, turned up, hoping to safeguard the social legislation for the workers which he had won by his support of the previous government.

Also present was Otilio Ulate, the man who had won the last presidential election, only to have it nullified by the crooked politicians. Though it was his election which had been overturned, he had refused to cooperate with the revolution in any way. Rather, he preferred to remain in San José and wait until he was rewarded by the efforts and the sacrifices of his fellow countrymen.

Various government representatives also showed up to swell the numbers, to get their pictures in the papers and to add to the confusion. They were overshadowed by a delegation of five foreign ambassadors, including our friend, the American ambassador, Nathaniel Davis. Their presence was designed to give a guarantee of international sanction to the proceedings so that the revolution would not look like just another palace coup. And finally, of course, there were Figueres, Chico Orlich and Alberto Marten.

Messages were carried back and forth to Teodoro Picado, the president, demanding unconditional surrender. At first these demands were unconditionally refused, and the revolutionary soldiers prepared to continue the fight. But before that could be carried out, Figueres decided to dispatch Father Nuñez to the capital to give the government one last chance before San José would be attacked.

The ambassadors accompanied Father Nuñez back to San José and decided to use the Mexican Embassy as a venue for the meetings of further negotiations. Each foreign diplomat went to his own embassy to communicate with the several governments. When they reassembled Ambassador Davis brought shocking news. In the midst of peace talks, President Picado had appealed to the Nicaraguan dictator, Somosa, for military help. Somosa had responded with an armed invasion of Costa Rica along its northern border; by the time word of this reached the Figueres forces, Nicaraguan troops had already invaded the northern province of Guanacaste. President Picado, in a last desperate attempt to save himself and his government, had turned to his country's traditional enemy.

But the attempt failed. Pressure from the American ambassador, from the Organization of American States, from representatives of various governments, and especially from the majority of Costa Rica's citizens proved too strong. The Nicaraguans withdrew, allowing the peace process to proceed.

Somehow, a surrender was arranged among them all—or perhaps, in spite of.

According to the terms of the agreement, the leading figures of the government would leave the country. That included both the president and the vice president, as well as various military leaders, the close colleagues of the party which had been in power, and the former president, Calderón Guardia, the main supporter of the Communist movement.

While the negotiations were going on, President Picado, Calderón Guardia, and a group of their henchmen left the country, taking with them as much government property as they could commandeer. They took over not only cars and trucks and road building equipment, but even went so far as to rip out the bathtubs and light fixtures from the Presidential House. Furniture from the President's residence, in addition to dishes, china, table linens and curtains were loaded into trucks and taken to Nicaragua, where the Costa Rican officials were warmly welcomed by Anastasio Somosa.

Along with many others I felt that the terms of the surrender agreement were too lenient. Most of us felt that harsher treatment of those who had abused their authority and had sent men to their death should be imposed on the guilty. However, those directly involved in the negotiations decided that the country needed an immediate peace more than anything else. There had been enough divisiveness, enough destruction to last everyone into the next decade. It was time for the healing process to begin.

The Revolution was over. Now our problems would really begin. We planned to set up a governing Junta with thirteen members, of which Pepe would be president. We had talked endlessly about organizing the Second Republic and about starting Costa Rica on a new path. Now, confronting it as inescapable reality, the prospect seemed indeed daunting. First and foremost, it entailed rooting out corruption. That would be followed by reforming the banking system, the public administration, the country's agricultural base, the educational system and finally, introducing a more technical approach to government. Since we would be in power for less than two years, the relentless pressure to bring about profound social change never let up.

Josef Stalin once said that diplomacy comes out of the barrel of a gun. We had achieved our first goal through a gun's barrel. Now we had to prove that we could govern.

Chapter XIII

The Victory Parade looked the way all parades should look: crowds packed along the sidewalks, the triumphant troops swinging down the avenue, the smiling leaders waving to the multitudes, beautiful girls tossing flowers in the brilliant sunshine. There were, of course, special Costa Rican twists. As the fighting men stomped along the Avenida Central nearly all of them were out of step because our troops weren't soldiers and had had no training in marching. Similarly, the bands had difficulty um-pah-pahing on the same beat since the instruments were rarely first quality and most of the musicians were Sunday players whose grasp of the finer points of rhythm was shaky at best. But nobody cared. The drummers whacked joyously away while everybody cheered everything, and Pepe's song was played over and over. As the wobbly lines of the parade moved forward I remembered the day I had met the man who was now president of the governing Junta and my aunt's improbable prophecy. Fittingly enough, that was the only prediction she ever made which turned out to be accurate. Some time later she said that she felt she had fulfilled part of her destiny in insisting that I had to link my life with Pepe's.

He appeared now with Chico Orlich and Alberto Marten, the three of them sitting together at the back of a jeep. They had been involved with each others' lives since childhood and it seemed appropriate that they should be riding together at this moment of triumph. Together they had planned the revolution, helped finance it, fought in it side by side, and were now enjoying the heady taste of victory. At that moment it would have been impossible to convince them that their cooperation would only be shared for a few more months before it tore apart.

Now, however, the day was inching along and finally the celebration was over. The last sky rocket had flared across the heavens, the last Viva Pepe! had been bellowed, and the last drink to the revolution had slid down someone's thirsty throat. And now it was time to get to work. To learn to administer the complexities of the state. To try to bring about reforms which were acceptable to enough people to win their support so that the changes in Costa Rican society could be implemented.

In the meantime, we had to find a place to live. Since the presidential house had been wrecked by Calderón Guardia's followers, we had no place else to go, so we moved into the large and comfortable home of our Canadian-Costa Rican friends, Alex Murray and his wife, Chichi. She was the daughter of the country's largest sugar producer. An Oxford University graduate, she was a woman wise in the culture of Costa Rica, and sophisticated about much of the rest of the world. Alex had studied Engineering at McGill University in Montreal. He had gone to England during the Second World War where he had been in charge of supplying the French Underground in their struggle against the Nazis.

So for three months we stayed with the Murrays. Complete with maids, nurses, guards, secretaries, chauffeurs and unknown hangers-on, we moved into the big house where Alex and Chichi turned over most of the top floor to our menage.

Painted pale yellow, the house was vaguely colonial in style with arches and flowering vines climbing over fences and up the side of the garage. Since the furniture had survived four Murray children, it was tough and seasoned, now covered with flowered chintz and blending its patterns with fresh roses produced by Chichi's green thumb. The water system of the house may have ante-dated Christopher Columbus for it never functioned well. It was impossible to take a shower and wash dishes at the same time because the pressure wasn't strong enough to lift the water up to the second floor except at restricted moments. In spite of that, though, the house reflected its owners and exuded a special warmth which enclosed us all. Its large living room windows were filled with sunlight all morning, and later with the curtains drawn at night, we enjoyed a coziness which I felt was always lacking in the homes of our Latin relatives and friends.

It was in the upper living room of the Murray house that the governing Junta held its first official meetings. A little ill at ease during the early stages, the new ministers of the Cabinet sat around the oblong coffee table in what had once been the Murray's nursery, and tried to make intelligent decisions. Bizarre and unreal as it seemed, they gradually realized that for now and for the foreseeable future, they were the only government their country had. And to add to the unreality, every now and then Chichi's voice, addressing her younger daughter, would float along the passage leading to their meeting room.

"Marigold! Get out of the shower at once! Mary is trying to wash dishes!" Mary, the wonderful Jamaican cook, presided over the kitchen. She not only produced home-made bread whose fragrance wafted through the house in the early morning, but also prepared for breakfast the best poached eggs this side of paradise. In addition, every afternoon at four o'clock the tea cart would appear, starched white linen napkins to spread over our laps to protect us from English marmalade and finger rolls so light I always felt they might float away up to the ceiling.

* * * * * * * *

For the next year and a half, Pepe governed with a Junta composed of thirteen men. They had been hand-picked by him and were successful businessmen or farmers. The exceptions were one priest, one schoolteacher, and Edgar Cardona, named Minister of Defense, who hadn't done much of anything except fight when he was needed. None had been in politics before. None had any interest in becoming a strongman in the Latin American sense of the term. At the

174

end of their months in office, they all cleaned out their ministerial desks and went back to their businesses or farms. Several years later, four or five returned to politics to win and lose elections.

From his first days in office, Pepe seemed perfectly at ease, as though he had been preparing for this all this life. And in a sense he had. Convinced that he was destined to lead, for years he had followed a disciplined regime of reading, studying, thinking about government problems, developing ideas and plans. He decided that one of his main tasks was to educate the public about society's dilemmas and to try to strip the solutions—as far as possible—from the pressures of politics. For this reason, he accepted almost every invitation to speak and used every forum as a platform from which to launch a series of lectures analyzing the country's problems and explaining the new government's policies to attempt to solve them.

As a kind of defense to cover what he feared were his inadequacies as head of state, he played the game of the peasant president. He was the leader who had always been so busy producing and creating that he had never taken time out to learn the sophisticated ways of the world. When someone once asked him why he didn't dance, his answer was his usual combination of truth and self deception.

"I couldn't do that. All that turning and turning makes me seasick." But the real reason was that he was too unsure of himself in social situations to get close enough to a woman to dance with her. He had no small talk and was never able to figure out how to relate to women at all—except as bed partners. So the facade of the peasant president was a shield behind which he hid. However, those who knew him were aware that the peasant president spoke five languages, Spanish, Catalán, English, German, French, and read Latin and some Greek. He was an agricultural expert, could write and speak with the sure touch of a professional, had become a successful businessman and was training himself to be adept at persuasion and negotiation.

But like many magnetic public figures, whether in the world of the theater or of politics, he was surprisingly shy when he was not front stage center in the place of honor. Unless he were talking to someone with superior knowledge of a subject whose brains he could pick, Pepe tended to retreat into himself and very soon to lose patience with the social whirl. In fact, on a personal level, he was never at ease in situations where people were just chatting, relaxing and having fun.

"I can't understand why they are willing to waste so much time!" he said as he once watched people at a fiesta. "I've been here twenty minutes and nobody's said anything intelligent yet!"

But I never felt that wasting time was his real objection. Rather, I wondered if the reason behind the reason he gave wasn't simply that in a situation where people were flirting and drinking, he couldn't dominate the conversation. At a fiesta nobody wanted to listen to a lecture about the brave new world we could create if we would all sacrifice as much as he had. If we dedicated ourselves to the task at hand, there would be paradise now! I gradually became convinced that he objected to parties because alcohol and sexual titillation did not form a fitting background for discussions about remaking society nearer to our heart's desire— or rather, his.

A continuing source of anxiety during the early months of government came from an unexpected quarter. Alberto Marten, his lawyer and oldest friend, objected from the beginning to many of the government's actions. Marten believed that bringing about profound social and economic change should be done with a meat cleaver: cut away the unwanted parts and ignore the shrieks of rage which you know will accompany any switch in the shifts of power. The sooner the better, and the deeper the cuts, the earlier the healing process can begin.

Pepe's approach was the exact opposite. He believed that winning the support of the large land owners and the more powerful financial groups would make any reforms the Junta wanted to bring about easier to implement. There would be less opposition and fewer enemies to have to contend with. In his discussions with Alberto he would plead for patience.

"If you would just exhibit some of that charm and flattery you show towards beautiful women, we could defuse the political opposition."

"You're deceiving yourself. We'll never win them. They're opposed to everything we want to do." Marten's voice, so soft and wooing when he wanted to be convincing, now had developed a warning rasp like a snake shaking its rattles. A proud man of swift and easy anger, Alberto did not suffer fools gladly and often seemed to look for the most abrasive way to express his ideas. "They'll never agree with us. So to hell with them!"

The two of them would go over and over their differences, never resolving anything and leaving every encounter in a growing state of rage. From Alberto's position the situation became increasingly difficult because most of the members of the Junta sided with Pepe, feeling that Marten's ideas were too extreme to be implemented. For his part, he was convinced that since none of the other ministers, except Father Nuñez, the Minister of Labor, had studied economics, their opinions were not worth listening to. And he did little to hide his contempt.

I would hear about the quarrels from Pepe and from the other members of the Junta. Though most of them admired Marten intellectually and were aware of his brilliance, they all wanted him to lower his rhetoric a little. They kept urging him not attack with such intensity and zeal anyone who opposed him, and to learn to shut up when their policies came under siege.

Chico summed it up. "Dammit, what we want is to win everybody's support, not just win the argument."

* * * * * * * *

Though Pepe announced repeatedly that he did not like to waste time in socializing, one social event he did enjoy: our first reception at the American Embassy. The official invitation arrived amid a flutter of mail, in the first bagful after the Junta had installed itself as the government. The card with the Great Seal of the United States of America was heavy, white and impressive, and it seemed to weigh down my hand with all the faith and credit of the U. S. government. Requesting the pleasure of our company at a reception honoring the President, José Figueres, and the Governing Junta of the Second Republic, the raised lettering informed us of the hour (seven pm), of the place (the Embassy) and of the fact that black tie was expected.

Pepe read the invitation two or three times and I could see that he was pleased. Being invited by the American Embassy so soon after the Junta had taken power gave the new government a legitimacy it would not have had even if it had been recognized by every other country in the world. But as he read the invitation once again, he seemed baffled by something.

"What does this mean? Why the black tie? It is not some kind of mourning, is it?"(For the death of a close relative, parent, child, sibling, Latin men wore a black tie for six months or longer.)

"No. That means you have to wear a tux."

"Tucks? That is something in sewing. Long ago I looked it up. The dictionary defined it as a small pleat or fold."

"This is a different word, different spelling. T U X, short for tuxedo. It's a black or dark suit a man wears on formal occasions. With a fancy shirt and a bow tie."

"Bow? Not with arrow?"

Oh, God, how long would we be mired down in this linguistic morass?

178

"Never mind. I'll go this afternoon and see if I can buy a tux in your size. Otherwise, you'll have to borrow one from somebody. There's no time to have one made." I left the house at once and tried to stay busy because this was my first official reception and I was becoming more and more nervous. I knew that people would hate my hair and make fun of anything I wore. Though I had been to the American Embassy before, it had always been accompanying my aunt and uncle and no one there had paid any attention to me. But now....

By the next evening I reflected that winning the Revolution was nothing. To move six hundred men through enemy lines carrying all their equipment either on their backs or on horses was as child's play compared to getting Pepe organized into a borrowed tuxedo. Since he had never worn one before, he was ill at ease and responded by whining and complaining without a pause. Everything he put on was uncomfortable and was either too small or too large. At first the shirt studs baffled him completely and then he dropped one which, of course, rolled under the bed. The cuff links were too big and heavy and pulled his cuffs too far down out of his jacket sleeves. Then he picked up the black, patent leather shoes. He turned them one way and then the other, his face slowly hardening with contempt. After a moment, he threw them back into the closet.

"I will not wear those shoes."

"Why not?" I asked, not really caring because by now the whole enterprise had become so exhausting I hated him. Anyway, it no longer seemed to matter: every passing minute increased my fears at the prospect of facing all the other guests who would probably make fun of me as soon as we entered the house.

"They are for the women. Like the sissies." Poking around on the closet floor he extracted something else, sat down on the bed and began to put them on.

"But those are what you ride horseback in!"

"No one will notice."

"Everyone will notice! This is a formal reception."

However, he had stopped listening and was now concentrating on his bow tie. Having never tied one before, he couldn't keep it centered correctly and finished by allowing it to list badly to port.

"To go through all this is idiotic. Why could I not just wear a regular dress?"

"Suit," I corrected. "In English, you use a different word. Dress is for women."

"Well, whatever it is, this one makes me look like a waiter. At the Embassy, everyone will be asking me to bring them a whiskey and soda."

Needless to say, at this point we were already twenty minutes late. But when he was finally ready, I turned him towards the mirror. "Have a look. That's what it's all about."

He stared at himself in the glass, stopping his complaints in mid sentence. I could see that he was entranced. Like a high school student at the Senior Prom wearing his rented tuxedo, the President of the Junta surveyed himself in the mirror, turning slowly this way and that, pulling the jacket down a little here, straightening his collar a little there. Even the black tie had decided to be cooperative and stood upright in the proper place. The total effect was impressive.

"Well," he said, turning slowly to get a better view of his reflection, "if they do think I am a waiter, I hope they will give me a big tip."

Still admiring himself in the mirror he indulged in one of his unexpected shifts in conversation, usually designed to throw people off balance.

"Do you know why I wanted you?" he suddenly demanded.

My heart fluttering, I waited, expecting a paean of praise for my beauty, brilliance, wit, charm and general uniqueness. "Well," he said, "there were three reasons." I wondered if he knew Elizabeth Barrett Browning well enough to recall

How do I love thee, let me count the ways? "There were three reasons: you don't paint your nails, you don't smoke and you speak English without an accent."

We arrived at the Embassy. By now I was used to being driven everywhere in a government car with a chauffeur and a plainclothes guard in the front seat, machine guns across their laps. Often an extra machine gun was left lying on the floor in the back and the children and I would have to push it aside as we fumbled our way onto the seat. We also got used to having one or two grenades in the glove compartment. As Muni was lifted into the car one day, she pointed at them and asked, "Is one of those the bomba atómica?"

I was even no longer surprised by the fact that most of the members of the Junta carried pistols in their belts. Though all hostilities had ceased, our family was still subjected to anonymous kidnapping threats, with both Martí and Pepe the targets. That meant that Martí was never permitted to be alone. An armed guard took him to school, walked him into the building and picked him up in the afternoon. I tried to play down the danger in explaining it to him, but for months and months he slept badly and became even more attached to me. As for Muni and me, being female, we were probably not at risk, for at that time Latins were still too chivalrous to harm women.

The American Embassy was an impressive, three-story, white house. Its sweeping colonial style was enhanced with porches on all sides, with heavy leaded glass windows and with chandeliers whose glitter flashed out into the gardens. As we approached the entrance we could see the ambassador anxiously watching the door, hoping the guest of honor would turn up before the ice melted and all the food developed salmonella. Then the band struck up the National Anthem as the ambassador spotted us and came forward, while all the other guests turned in our direction like flowers following the sun.

Though I was nearly thirty, I was still sometimes attacked by waves of shyness which made me freeze with self-consciousness and occasionally even blush. Adding to my discomfort was an inability to decide what to do with my hands. No matter what I tried they became heavier and heavier, hanging lower and then lower still until I felt that my fingernails must be nearly scratching the floor. Could I be elected Miss Urangutang of the Second Republic?

Now, as the anthem played on and on, promising to last longer than a Wagnerian opera, we all stood motionless while I felt every eye glued to my front, critical, mocking, full of derision. I was suffocating as the temperature oozed higher and higher. Shy people never think that observers are consumed with admiration or envy; rather, those watching eyes reflect only contempt covered by a brittle courtesy. I longed for the day when self-assurance could be bottled in small vials like perfume, and then before every public appearance I would be able to pour a few drops down my throat for spiritual fortification. Since the drops were not available now however, I had to wait until at least ten people assured me that my dress was stunning, my hair organized into the proper swirls and my earrings elegant enough to be protected by the constitution before I could relax sufficiently to enjoy all the sparkle and brilliance.

Ambassador Nathaniel Davis had the grace to look the part. He was impressively tall and with enough of a stomach to be considered attractive, because at that time Latins still equated the lean and hungry look with either disease or malnutrition. Now he raised his glass.

"To the brave men who won the Revolution. To the ancient friendship of our two countries. And to the success of the new president who has so admirably proven his dedication to democracy and freedom."

We solemnly raised our glasses of champagne and drank, then turned towards Pepe hoping his response would not lead to another lecture about the Junta's plans for the new Costa Rica.

Absent-minded as always when he was about to speak in public, Pepe couldn't decide what to do with his empty glass. He looked around for a table on which to abandon his goblet but couldn't find one close enough. Finally, smiling graciously, he handed it to the Papal Nuncio (the personal representative of the Pope), perhaps with the hope that it would be snatched up to heaven by divine intervention. Then he took a step forward.

"Ladies and gentlemen," he began," in the name of the Junta and of—"

But he was interrupted. A waiter in a white coat was suddenly beside him, his face split from side to side in a smile which showed every one of his gold teeth.

"Pepe!" he bellowed, "No puedo creer! Carajo, hombre!! Tanto gusto de verte!" He swung his tray of drinks from side to side, needing some kind of furniture on which to unburden himself so that he could shake hands. Since no table appeared, he swiveled once more and came face to face with the ambassador whom, of course, he did not recognize. He shoved the glasses forward.

"Tome, Señor, con permiso," he said, and handed him the tray.

Caught by surprise, the ambassador clung to his burden which tilted precariously as the glasses started sliding toward one edge, the alcohol sloshing over and slowly beginning to form puddles on the silver tray. The waiter turned towards the president of the Junta.

"Pepe! Como estás? Yo soy Juan Fernandez. En la escuela primaria, hombre!"

"Juan! Juan Fernandez!" They flung their arms around each other, both talking at once as they grinned and grinned, pounding each other on the back and beginning to reminisce. "Remember that time Chico Orlich put the rotten mango in the math teacher's chair."

"You're damn right I remember! And I remember how you always argued with the teacher about the Spanish Civil War. And now you're president! I sure as hell never thought you'd amount to a goddam thing."

More abrazos and more memories followed amid loud bursts of laughter as the President of the Junta slid back to the Second Grade and for a few moments became happily involved in a world of practical jokes, boyhood vulgarities and that time they played hooky for two whole days and didn't get caught. Politically astute enough to realize the value of the moment, he pretended to forget the ambassador and the elegant guests while he and the waiter renewed their grammar school friendship.

My memory is hazy but I think it may have been the Papal Nuncio, the Dean of the Diplomatic Corps, who finally brought the party back. Touching the presidential sleeve with ecclesiastical deftness, he remonstrated softly.

"Señor Presidente, el embajador está esperando."

Since the ambassador was waiting, suddenly the scene reverted to what it had been before Juan Fernandez came into our lives. He picked up his tray of drinks, the president straighten his tie, the ambassador looked deferential, and the ritual moved forward.

As I smiled and smiled nearly developing a nervous tick, I reflected that courage was such a contradictory quality. Shaking every hand that came near me, I remembered that during the Revolution I had been prepared to walk two hundred kilometers through freezing mountain passes to escape to Panama, but here I was afraid to face a room full of people who might not like the way my hair was done. Those watchful, unblinking eyes frightened me more than cold or endless walking, and it was several years before I could convince myself that in general people were too involved with themselves to notice much of what was happening around them. Greeting each guest with my stiff, official smile, I tried to say something personal. If they asked, I also tried to remember what the government's policy was regarding the poor banana workers, the rich coffee growers, and the in-between business people. Since we were so newly installed, the government had no policy yet about many issues so I could retreat behind a phrase such as "still under consideration" when anyone asked me something I didn't know.

During a pause Chico Orlich, the Minister of Public Works, strode over to me. He and Pepe couldn't remember when they hadn't known each other, a relationship deepened by the fact that not only were they related by marriage but for several years had also been business partners. Chico's attitude was that of an older brother, humorous and a little protective.

Resembling his Yugoslav ancestors with light brown hair and eyes and a skin lined by the sun, he would have been at home in a ship sailing up and down the Dalmatian coast. Named Minister of Public Works, Chico was the kind of collaborator who should have been put into mass production because he never created problems. A pragmatic, hard-working man, he rarely engaged in theoretical discussions but instead, devoted himself to finding practical solutions to whatever tangle lay at hand. As a successful coffee producer, he was used to dealing with the day-to-day complications of the growing, harvesting and marketing of the country's leading export crop. He was the perfect choice as Minister of Public Works. Now he came straight to the point like one of his family's sea captains following the compass to the north.

"Why the hell did you let him wear those shoes? He should have given them to a coffee picker ten years ago. Everybody thinks he's crazy!"

I started to explain, but decided that it was too late. "Maybe that's what he really wants. He says that being considered mad gives you a lot of freedom. People don't expect you to act like everybody else."

As the evening was ending, Father Nuñez, the new Minister of Labor, reached the outside door just ahead of us. An expert in labor relations, he had studied in the United States and represented the liberal wing of Costa Rica's Catholic church. Coming from a peasant family, he was proud of the fact that his father was a barefooted oxman who earned his livelihood hauling loads of coffee and black beans to the local market. Nuñez had gone into the church as his one means of moving up and out.

Now I realized that this was the first time I had seen him in his formal, diplomatic garb. It was jet black from head to toe, and was covered by a scarlet cape which blew out behind him in a dramatic, crimson cloud. Even without his cape though, he always reminded me of Mephistopheles: the glittering black eyes looking deep into yours as he smiled his little smile full of your darkest secrets, the ones he knew you couldn't bear anyone ever finding out.

Realizing that we were catching up, he stepped aside and waved us forward. His sweeping flourish needed only a plumed hat to look like D'Artagnan of The Three Musketeers. Just as we reached the door he caught up with us and leaned forward in a conspiratorial pose, his eyes flicking about to see if anyone else were listening. The low voice had a unecclesiastical edge.

"Thank God the Papal Nuncio is slightly deaf," he said, "and didn't hear Juan's remarks. That language of his sounded pretty racy, even for the ears of a churchman."

Chapter XIV

Part of my duties in playing the diplomatic social game was entertaining ambassadors and their wives when they came for formal calls. In the centuries before the communications revolution ambassadors carried out important duties for their rulers, representing them in negotiations, taking secret messages back and forth, supplying information about military or social conditions, stirring up religious, romantic or financial trouble when the situation warranted it. But the telephone made ambassadorial duties ever more irrelevant; if one head of state needed to communicate with another, he picked up the phone and discussed the problem directly. In Costa Rica in the 1940s and 1950s however, the ambassadors still carried out their duties which were largely ceremonial and were principally in the realm of public relations.

One day after Pepe had left for the Presidential House the phone rang. It was the Embassy of the United Kingdom. The ambassador and his wife were asking permission to call on the wife of the new president of the Junta.

These calls followed a rigid formula which applied both to professional and personal visits. If the husband and wife came together, they left cards on a silver tray in the entrance hall of their hosts, one card with the wife's name, two cards with the husband's. My aunt had enlightened me before my marriage.

"The wife leaves only one card because she calls only on the señora of the house, while the husband calls both on the señor and the señora. And if you are not at home they leave the cards, bending up one corner to indicate that they have come personally. But if they have sent the chauffeur with flowers or a gift or just a greeting, then the cards are not bent."

It all seemed so byzantine and arcane I was baffled at trying to give the bend or not to bend the importance it seemed to merit.

The British ambassador and his wife were the first of a parade of diplomats who came in an endless file to present their good wishes and their government's hope for our success. As a rule these visits were mercifully brief. The English diplomat was gracious, smooth as silk and ever so slightly bored with life in what he considered a banana republic. And ditto his wife. He looked like a heavier version of Lord Byron without all the sexual antennae quite so aflutter, while she could have been a model for a Pre-Raphaelite painting, pale and poetically delicate. They were too experienced, however, to let their boredom or anything else show on the surface. In fact, they both presented a facade worthy of the empire on which the sun was just beginning to set.

They arrived at exactly five o'clock on a rainy afternoon. Since this was my first diplomatic call, I was very nervous, wondering what to say, wondering if there were subjects I should avoid, wondering if the government of Great Britain, Ireland and the Dominions Beyond the Seas had any special relations with Costa Rica to which I should obliquely refer. In a country with a properly organized Foreign Office I would have been briefed on relations with each country whose representatives were coming to call. But at that period in Costa Rica's history everything was still so higgeldy-piggeldy after the Revolution, and even before, that I was left solely on my own.

But I needn't have worried. Both my guests were so relieved at not having to speak Spanish (like good Anglo-Saxons they believed that if you wanted to speak to them, learn English), they outdid themselves in "oozing charm from every pore," and the visit went off handsomely.

Having read somewhere that diplomats drank sherry, I began by offering them a glass.

After a tiny pause the ambassador said, "Uh, that would be very nice."

And she added, "Yes, very."

It wasn't until some weeks later that I learned that he drank only Scotch and she, vodka, but on this occasion, they made do. Settling back into our chairs we women waited, as befitted our secondary position in society, for the ambassador to begin the conversation. "I find life in Latin America quite enjoyable. My government feel that we've done very well in helping economic development go forward in this part of the world."

"Yes," I agreed, "I understand that the railroad down to the Atlantic was financed by English money. I came up on that train when I first arrived from the States."

"Same thing in Argentina, you know. And much of the beef industry, too."

He took a sip of his drink with what seemed to me a proprietary air. It was true that before American money had moved into Latin America, the British had ranged far and wide in their business ventures, financing roads, dams, coffee production, and communications systems in a dozen countries north and south of the Equator.

"You have some very interesting chaps here in the government," the ambassador went on. "I was attending a political meeting recently, and afterwards, as we were having drinks, two of them began reciting poetry!"

He would have had his tongue cut out before admitting it, but he was disconcerted about the kind of men he would be dealing with in the Costa Rican government. Used to facing primitive caciques in Central America wearing their jackboots and pistols, the diplomats now confronted a governing Junta made up of some members as highly educated as themselves. Several of the ministers had advanced degrees, many had read widely in economic and social theory, and almost all were skilled in various areas of their country's agricultural and professional life.

As I listened to those flutey voices I remembered Alex Murray's tales about his years in England during the Second World War. Using some of the skills he had acquired in supplying the French Underground, he took charge of our communications during the weeks of our fighting in the mountains. He would either carry messages himself through enemy lines or else devise ingenious ways to get word through.

"This is the most fun I've had since the War. And a lot less dangerous. Fortunately, dealing with Costa Ricans is not exactly the same thing as the German Wehrmacht."

Under Alex's guidance peasants would turn up every now and then with a message buried under a load of black beans. Once or twice he sent papers attached to the under part of an oxcart's yoke with the number of new government recruits and where they were bound for. From the earliest days of the struggle Alex arranged for a network of ham radio operators to send and receive information in a code he made up. He organized the group so that someone would always be on duty and would be able to transmit information to all parts of the country. Endlessly imaginative, he was tireless in keeping the messages flowing back and forth, never at a loss for new ways to maintain contact if one of the avenues was closed off. Fearless and dedicated, Murray was the kind of champion every movement needed—especially cherished because he came unencumbered by any delusions of grandeur.

As I grew more accustomed to the diplomatic minuet, I discovered that husbands and wives who worked the international circuits developed little signals to help each other through the ordeal of visits. Now, as Mrs. Ambassador was talking, out of the corner of my eye I saw his Excellency glance surreptitiously at his watch and take the last sip from his glass, which he then set down on the table with a tiny clink.

"And I was just getting ready to go the Henley Regatta when—" But at the sound of the clink she stopped her story in mid- sentence, and began to gather up her white gloves and silk purse. I decided that that must be the signal, for they rose simultaneously as though pulled by invisible ropes, and began moving towards the door in a smooth, well oiled maneuver working their way out amid a shower of goodbyes as they disappeared down he steps under their umbrellas.

* * * * * * * *

Most of these visits went off without mishap for the diplomatic call was as stylized as a ballet. But occasionally disaster struck. The French ambassador came not long afterwards, frightfully proper, a member of a hoity-toity French family with a pedigree going back to Charlemagne. He looked deceptively young with slicked back dark hair and an aristocratic nose, and he tried hard not to be too obvious about letting me know that he was expecting a much better post as soon as he had done time in Central America. I felt in my stomach that hot jab of resentment which comes when someone is being patronizing and all the responses you can think of are too vulgar to express. Since his Spanish was worse than my French we were having a hard time of it until there was an interruption.

Along one wall of the living room the wide staircase to the second and third floors swept up majestically to a landing, then turned right for a farther rise to a hall leading to the bedrooms. A noise on the landing, followed by a child's laughter, then squeals and rapid footsteps made me look up. My daughter's four-year-old dirty face peered through the bannisters.

"Mommy, I'm going to have my bath now." And still squealing, she raced down the stairs, stark naked, making straight for the ambassador. But instead of drawing the perfectly pressed diplomatic trousers away, he put out one manicured hand and took her grimy fingers in his. Seemingly at ease for the first time since he had arrived, he smiled happily and leaned forward in his chair.

"Hello," she said. "I'm Muni. Who are you?"

"Oh, you speak English. That is easier for me. I am François."

"Do you want to take a bath with me?"

But before her invitation could be accepted, there came the bump, bump of wooden wheels followed almost at once by what sounded like the baaing of a goat. Was it a children's phonograph record? One of the guards playing with the kids and entertaining them with animal sounds? And why had the nurse, Lila, permitted them to be running up and down the stairs at visiting hours?

The bump-bump got louder, the baaing increased and now there came the clack-clack of—not hooves! I glance up in time to see two small horns rounding the corner of the landing and starting down the stairs. At the look on my face the French ambassador dropped Muni's hand and whirled around in his chair. Baaing steadily, a small brown-and-white goat skipped down the steps dragging a tiny goat-cart behind, my son, Martí, holding the reins and roaring with delight.

I jumped up and the ambassador rose also. All pretense of an official visit had now evaporated as Martí and the goat ricocheted around the room, his and the animal's bellows mixing in a rising crescendo. Swaying wildly, the goat-cart crashed into chairs and upset two small tables, one with an ashtray and a crystal cigarette box which splintered on the floor. Muni, standing tiptoe on a coffee table, contributed piercing shrieks of delight which raised the noise level to a pitch high enough to shatter glass.

In two seconds I reached the door leading to the servants passage.

"Lila! Come at once! Giusseppe! Come! All of you! Bring the guards!"

In no time the living room was crammed with people. Complete with their rifles two guards charged in, followed by Lila and another maid, and then

Giusseppe, the houseboy. Everybody talked at once, issuing orders and contradicting them, getting in each other's way, tripping over the guns as the guards flung themselves on the terrified goat and tried to extract Martí from the cart.

"No!" he bellowed, "I want to ride some more!"

"Martí, get out of that cart right now, dammit!" Then I turned to the guards and pointed to the goat. "Out! Outside! Don't ever let this happen again!"

One guard scooped up the goat and the other, the cart. They were both country fellows and couldn't understand why the señora didn't want a cute little goat in her living room.

"How did he come in?" I demanded, still outraged.

"Yai, Señora," the older guard said, "the little ones wanted the goat upstairs in the playroom. Up on the third floor. So me and Manuel took him up there." It was said so casually, so matter of factly, they might have been talking about taking a newspaper up to the sun room.

Finally, after the doors had opened and closed twenty-eight times, they had all left. They had taken the goat and the cart and the guards and the guns and the three servants, and every last one of them had disappeared. Everybody.

Exhausted, I slid down into a chair, thankful to be alone. The healing silence drifted around the room, a gossamer cloud closing out noises and voices and all demands for attention. I could feel my nerve endings beginning to unwind as I sank back into the comfort of a soundless place where nothing moved, where for a few precious moments no one required a single thing of me or insisted on an instant solution to any problem.

In the soothing silence a voice sounded.

"You have forgotten me."

I turned. There, leaning back in a corner of the sofa, sat the French ambassador. Startled and resentful, I stared at him wishing he were dead—or at least that he had the grace to be a deafmute. Perhaps he realized how tired I was for after a moment he stood up and came forward, smiling and at ease, and I became aware that in some magical way, His Excellency, the Ambassador of the French Republic, had metamorphosed into plain François.

"This has been a visit, Madame, I shall always cherish, the most charming one of my entire diplomatic career."

We were moving towards the door now and he stopped to kiss my hand.

"By the way, how old is your daughter.?"

"She's just turned four."

"Ah, then please tell her that in another fifteen years I shall be enchanted to accept her invitation."

The weeks moved forward bringing the train of diplomatic visits puffing steadily along. Since these encounters only lasted fifteen minutes I could accommodate more than one in an afternoon and learned to become quite fleet of foot in walzing couples first in and then out if they were not on the same political side and would rather not confront each other in such close quarters as our living room.

It was perhaps fitting that our most dramatic incident happened when the Italian ambassador and his signora were calling. Our cook, Giullietta, was from Italy, an emotional, fiery woman given to loud lamentations when things weren't going well, and convinced that all the world should know about it if life were not moving along as she had planned. Her husband's name was Giusseppe. He served the table, did much of the heavy cleaning, and was as cool and controlled as she was volatile. Together the Giulis, as we called them, looked after the kitchen and the food, her only demand being that she have a free hand about what to prepare for meals; she had at least five thousand fancy menus towards which she felt a deep moral obligation, and she would not tolerate any interference from me or any one else. Since I had resolutely refused to learn to cook because servants could do it all so much better, this arrangement suited me perfectly, and we rocked along amid peace and harmony as succulent meals appeared on schedule interrupted by only an occasional rumble from the volcanic Giulletta.

The Italian ambassador, Dr. Flavio Aldo and his wife spoke fluent Spanish, but with the musical intonation of their native language so that much of their conversation made me wonder if at any moment they might burst into song. Now he launched into a description of a recent vacation spent in Yellowstone National Park. "Ah, las flores, las montañas, el aire fresco, el río! impossible describir el escenario!"

As he talked, everything about him seemed to be in motion; his eyebrows bounced between heaven and hell while his flowing gestures outlined the mountains and valleys of the Park as his voice rose and fell in poetic cadences of crescendo and diminuendo. To my relief this visit seemed to be going swimmingly, for ever since the goat incident I had always felt a little tense about every visit until the goodbyes had been pronounced.

Among Giullietta newest creations were some hot spicy cheese straws which captivated all our guests and probably did more to cement our international relations than any treaty we could have negotiated. If she were in a good mood she would send the cheese straws in at exactly the right temperature, but if she were angry about something, they would arrive so smoking hot they were untouchable. Without thinking I offered the ambassador some. Still talking, he picked three or four, but as soon as his fingers closed over the tidbits, he let out what could only have been a classic Italian curse. And then bellowed, "Who is trying to incinerate me? I have done no harm to anyone!"

Oh, God, I thought, Giullietta is on the warpath. She's probably found out that Giusseppe is lusting after the new maid.

Just as I was about to ask if the ambassador's fingers needed medical attention, the door snapped open and Giusseppe flew across the room. He was running so fast his feet seemed to blend into a solid streak of black trousers topped by a white coat. Noiseless as a shadow, he flitted up the steps and disappeared.

For a moment Ambassador Aldo stopped talking. His glance riveted on the stairs up which Giusseppe had soared as he groped for an explanation. He turned to me and with one hand made a gesture of bafflement so graphic I could hear the Italian equivalent of what-the-hell-is-happening. (His other hand, its fingers still red from the burn, was hors de combat).

As though to answer, there was a scuffling at the door and Giulletta roared in. Trailing her came Lila and another maid who were clinging to either side trying vainly to hold her back. She shrugged them off, however, like someone slipping out of a coat, and went on with her work, sharpening a meat cleaver which clanked with a metallic click each time the file struck the blade, snicker-snack. Though she stopped short near the door her voice reverberated around the room, and in her rage she reverted to her native tongue.

"Dov e il bastardo?"

However shaky a grasp her listeners had on Italian, nobody had a communications problem with that question. We all began to respond at the same time.

"No, Giulletta," I began. "He's not here.!"

"He's gone! "The ambassador contributed, calling logic to his help. "As you can see, he's left."

Mrs. Ambassador joined the chorus and along with the maids we combined our voices. "He's probably outside. Not here.!"

Fuming, Giulletta glared around as though she suspected that we were hiding him under the sofa. And as she looked, the file and the cleaver clashed continually together, snicker-snack, her strokes getting faster and angrier. Then, volcano-like, she began to sputter a variety of maledictions in which the word for death erupted over and over. Her eyes fastened on each of us in turn checking to see if she could read in our faces where il bastardo had secreted himself. After a moment though, she turned away and stopped honing the meat cleaver long enough to test the blade with her thumb, a blade which by now must have had a cutting edge sharp enough to decapitate a hippopotamus.

In the silence there suddenly sounded the creak of a step. Flinging her head up she glanced towards the staircase and then, half crouching, she slowly began to tiptoe towards the bottom of the steps. Mesmerized, the maids and the diplomats stayed motionless, incapable of making a move or saying a word. Perhaps we were all thinking the same thing: she's going to slice him open with that meat cleaver and wrench his heart out with her bare hands.

Just as I was about to gather myself together enough to tell her to leave the room at once, there was a clatter of footsteps. As we watched, a large white pillow flew down the steps and banged into the cook's face. Giusseppe's voice flew right behind.

"Giullietta! Mi amore! You don't understand! You are the one I really love!"

And then Giusseppe himself flew after the words. In wild leaps he catapulted down the last ten steps below the landing and charged across the room towards the kitchen passage and the safety of the side garden. Giullietta staggered back from the shock of the heavy pillow and lost her balance so that she sagged against the back of a chair, dropping the meat cleaver with a loud bang.

But almost at once she recovered.

"Bastardo!" she roared at Giusseppe's retreating back. And since she had no other weapon she flung the file, rage lending strength to her arm. Fortunately she was a better chef than marksman for the file turned end over end, wobbled a little and then crashed harmlessly against the door. Giusseppe had survived the first assault.

I stood up and walked towards her. I felt that if we had reached the stage of flying objects it was time to declare a truce, at least until the foreign guests could be escorted out.

"Giullietta, go into the kitchen at once. We'll talk about Giusseppe later." Still fuming and still muttering, she turned to leave. "And take the file and the meat cleaver with you."

By now the ambassador had risen. Somewhat warily he eyed Giullietta, even more warily as she stooped to pick up the file and the cleaver. Signaling to his signora by shooting his eyebrows up to heaven, he began to edge towards the door, determined to preserve to the end the classic Roman qualities of courage and dignity. I waited at the exit for the diplomats to go down the steps to the street and was turning back into the house when I overheard a strange conversation.

"Signore Embajador!" came an urgent whisper.

The ambassador looked around for the disembodied voice. He was baffled, unable to figure out where the sound was coming from. Turning this way and that he finally spotted Giusseppe concealed among the thick bushes near the wrought iron gate.

"What do you want?"

"Signore embajador, please! She is going to kill me!"

"But what do you want me to do?"

"Take me with you! I can't stay here!"

198

For a moment the ambassador hesitated. Then he addressed the row of bushes, for by now Giusseppe had shifted his position and was completely hidden by the foliage.

"The car will be back in twenty minutes. Climb over the fence. I'll speak to the chauffeur."

The diplomat moved swiftly across the wide sidewalk to join his wife waiting at the car. Without looking around he said something to the driver who stepped forward to open the door. The Italians slid into the big black limousine which eased away from the curb as soon as they were seated.

We never saw Giusseppe again.

Chapter XV

Almost as soon as they were installed, the Junta began to carry out a host of fundamental reforms. First and most shocking was the nationalization of the banking system. Pepe wanted more credit available to the small producers of basic foodstuffs and to farmers growing coffee or bananas (export products on which the country's economic life depended). If that meant less credit to those who wanted to import expensive Scotch and large Cadillacs, so be it. Since the criteria of the private banks were to lend money mainly to those who were engaged in lucrative commerce, the country's limited amounts of credit were too often siphoned off into the luxury trades rather than going into needed production. The nationalization of the banks was an attempt to redress that situation.

Needless to say these measures aroused opposition among the well-to-do, many of whom were stockholders in the private banks. They were convinced that Figueres had betrayed them by his reforms. Used to the traditional way of controlling the country through their financial power, they realized early on that the Junta was embarked on a process which would increasingly curtail their economic clout. Every morning they would open the newspaper to see what other dreadful deed the Junta had perpetrated the previous day. And after reading the reports, the landowners and the big merchants would telephone each other and whine and moan.

"We should have stuck to Calderón!" they stormed. "This Figueres is worse than the communists! He wants us to pay our workers higher wages!"

"He's even talking about an income tax!"

"He's going to ruin us!"

The second effort to shift government help towards those of greatest need was to establish an Office of Price Control on basic foodstuffs. Rice, beans, sugar, lard, coffee, dried milk were the six indispensable foods of the average household. When prices were low, the Ministry of Agriculture would buy up foods so as to keep a supply on hand for releasing into the market when recurring periods of shortage drove the prices up. Since the peasant population lived close to the edge of hunger during much of the year, they needed to be protected against the upward spiral of food costs. As always with government agencies, it was difficult at first to find managers capable of making the organization function efficiently. No one had had the necessary experience or was sufficiently adroit in the political rough waters of the times to handle the opponents of the project. Of course there were the usual cries that it wouldn't work, that the food would spoil, be eaten by insects, fall prey to thieves, be sold for too low a price. And at one time or another, all these disasters occurred.

But gradually the techniques were developed to make the agency operate smoothly, and today, forty years later, the Office of Price Control is a going concern which helps stabilize the price of food.

* * * * * * * *

Meanwhile the controversy with Marten sizzled along. On the surface it was about how to approach the problems of carrying out social and economic reforms. How fast to go. How much to antagonize those used to positions of authority. But underneath, the struggle between the two men was really about power. Alberto was the only person in the Junta who was Pepe's intellectual equal and probably felt from the beginning that he should share more fully in decision making. But though the other ministers respected his brilliance he was so abrasive that they tended to listen carefully to his ideas but to take their cue about supporting him from Pepe's responses.

In meetings of the Junta Pepe's theme usually was to urge the ministers to make haste slowly. "If we try to go too far too fast, we'll simply doom ourselves to a backlash. And that will make any further social advances impossible."

Marten's response too often was only slightly concealed contempt. "You seem more courageous with a gun than with social policy."

By now they had reached that stage of disagreement where their misunderstandings blinded each to anything the other wanted to do. Both were convinced that his friend was not only mistaken but that the policies being advocated would lead to certain disaster. They left every meeting now with both men feeling hurt and angry. The situation rocked along growing increasingly strained as no solution could be found.

* * * * * * * *

In another area the Junta faced a simmering rage which proved difficult to deal with. After eight years of watching their society disintegrate, many people demanded that those responsible be forced to pay, or at least be publicly disgraced. While Pepe understood and sympathized with that feeling, he wanted to avoid a repetition of the vengeance which the French had shown as they hunted down and either killed or drove away those who had collaborated with the Nazis. He faced a relatively large group whose attitude was expressed by one man who said, "The only thing I can't forgive Figueres is that he didn't hang a Calderonista from every lamp post in the country."

Trying to defuse some of this animosity, the Junta used every opportunity to urge people to put the past behind. Whenever a minister spoke to any organization, he pleaded with his listeners to concentrate on rebuilding their society rather than in seeking an unsatisfying revenge. The ministers pointed out that too much psychic energy was being frittered away in keeping alive old hatreds. Instead, the government wanted to use its influence to move as many followers as possible towards the kind of political healing which would come from increasing productivity. It was a different twist on the adage, don't get mad, get even. Rather, the Junta said, don't get even, get busy.

In the economic field, a change which at first irritated many people was a new employment policy. The government began to hire only those who were qualified for the job rather than following an age-old custom of taking on whoever was somebody's brother, son or widow. A form of civil service was begun which winnowed prospective workers through examinations.

One example concerned Pepe's own brother, Antonio. In many Latin countries the president, to guarantee his own security, often appointed his brother to be Minister of Internal Security or Minister of the Interior, a post which controlled the armed forces. Instead, Pepe named someone else, Edgar Cardona, a man who had fought with him during the Revolution—an appointment which later proved to be a mistake. When people would ask Antonio why he was not participating in the Junta's activities or had not been given an important position, Antonio had a stock answer.

"There's no reason for me to have a job in this government. I'm not a politician. In fact, I don't know any more about what's going on in this Junta than I do about the government of Outer Mongolia." While the new employment policy antagonized many because it cut them off from the possibility of getting an easy job, gradually the wisdom of the change penetrated through the society and became more and more widely accepted.

An ever widening stream of reforms flowed out during the eighteen months of the Junta's administration. One of the most significant dealt with health care for the society as a whole. Pepe's attitude was summed up in one of his favorite sentences: "If too many man-hours of labor are lost through illness, no society can prosper. Therefore, caring for the primary health needs of all our citizens is a fundamental responsibility of government."

The Social Security system provided the most efficient method for solving the problem. Slowly its services were extended to greater and greater numbers of the population and slowly the protection reached out to cover the unemployed, the old, the disabled, the orphaned children, the homeless. In the coming years the services expanded to offer total health care for all citizens. Though it did not happen overnight, any needed operation was eventually available at public expense to the poorest person in society. As time passed, complete surgical, dental, orthopedic, obstetrical, pediatric and ophthalmological services were, bit by bit, provided to every citizen.

With the exception of a few small, private clinics, all hospitals and all doctors were incorporated into the Social Security system. Patients could go to government hospitals and receive health services at no expense; or they could go to private doctors who would charge them whatever the market would bear. Like higher education in all fields, medicine was financed at government expense. Therefore all doctors, after their years of schooling paid for from the public treasury, owed society a year's work in remote rural parts of the country. They were assigned to small health clinics which were set up in outlying areas to provide primary care to the best of their abilities. They usually had to work under fairly primitive conditions and many of them did not bring to their tasks the dedication of an Albert Schweitzer. But at least they provided minimum care to people who had never had a chance to see a doctor before in their lives. After the physician's social debt had been paid, he or she was permitted to move into town and to begin a regular medical practice.

The problems involving agriculture were as complicated as any which the Junta had to face. Though Costa Rica was an agricultural country, the distribution of land was less of a burning issue than it was in other, more feudal societies. Land in Costa Rica was and still is widely distributed. There are few huge estates covering thousands of acres such as are found in many South American countries. What agriculture needed in Costa Rica was technical help. It needed higher quality seed for the basic foods of corn and beans, better fertilizers and pest control, greater diversification of products, more efficient management of drainage and contour farming so that the torrential downpours of the Rainy Season did not wash away all the rich topsoil away.

Over a period of time most of these changes came about. Since Pepe had been a farmer for twenty years, he was aware of the myriad problems which country people face in the production of food or cash crops. His personal experience prevented the pursuit of pie-in-the-sky solutions to intractable problems, and his intimate acquaintance with peasants provided him with a vocabulary with which to address them. In talking with him they felt that they were communicating with someone who, though perhaps not exactly on their own level, at least was not a silly city slicker who didn't know how to help pull an oxcart out of the mud.

A few months after our marriage, Pepe, some peasants and I were on our way to Santa Elena to check on the coffee beneficio. Walking at the back of our group was a peasant whose yoke of oxen were pulling his cart full of corn to sell to the country store at Santa Elena. After we had traveled about two hours on the up-and-down country roads, the oxman stopped and began undoing the leather thongs holding the yoke to the animals' heads.

"What's he doing?" I asked.

Pepe turned to the oxman to find out why we were stopping.

"Yai, I have to change them from one side to the other. If not, they'll get bored."

The oxman and I smiled at each other. He was happy that Don Pepe was a farmer like him, and understood perfectly the problem of oxen's getting bored.

And I was happy that changing oxen from one side of the yoke to the other no longer seemed strange.

The reforms were by and large successfully carried out because Pepe had a clear idea of where he wanted the society to go. Over the years various organizations, some private, some public, had held monthly meetings and discussions analyzing the country's problems. One of the most prestigious was lead by the Rector of the University of Costa Rica, Dr. Rodrigo Facio. An economist and a scholar, he had shepherded a group of interested citizens in months of study, and had published a series of reports. These books, pamphlets and brochures presented possible solutions to some of the country's dilemmas. Probably few other Latin countries had had such an extensive review of how to deal with their national problems. Many of the answers had already been suggested. Many had to be improvised to fit the political realities of the times. Other solutions needed to be tailored to the theories which Pepe had been envisioning before and during his years of exile and which he was determined to implement now that he was in power.

Since the government had changed, however, nothing in Costa Rica could be done through force or imposition. Rather, reforms had to be carried out by discussion, argument and persuasion. There were no Stalinesque characters with guns forcing peasants to starve by the thousands in order to carry out a government plan for agriculture. No torture, no secret prison cells, no knocks on the door at three o'clock in the morning. No bullet in the back of the head.

But how they did talk, the irate citizens of Costa Rica! And write to the newspapers. And pontificate on the radio. And organize protest meetings. And issue manifestos.

To our satisfaction, however, only small numbers of people engaged in those obstructionists tactics. For in general, the Junta enjoyed wide-spread support. Most of the middle class was enthusiastic. As for the two largest groups in the country, the peasants who made up fifty per cent of the population, and the day laborers, there was no doubt where their sympathies lay. They were solidly behind the government.

All the time that Pepe was in politics, he was also a businessman, carrying on an ever expanding enterprise based in La Lucha. Though he was a superb politician, superior to any Costa Rican in this century, as a businessman he was something of a disaster. One of his major deficiencies was his refusal to learn how to become an administrator. He detested routine of any kind and was constantly experimenting to try to find better ways to do things. This lead to what amounted almost to a compulsion forcing him to start out in one direction, change his mind in mid stream, make spontaneous decisions, do an about-face, double back on himself and then scrap the whole project to start out on a new and more expensive tack. No one working with him was ever quite sure that the decisions made today would hold tomorrow.

One of his peculiarities was a tendency to fall in love with some one he worked with, usually someone foreign or trained in a foreign country. Not of course in a physical sense, because there was never any doubt about his sexual preferences. But every now and then he would become attached to employees and show a blindness which bordered on the irrational. It made him incapable of admitting their defects, or in a few cases their outright crookedness. Frequently he would follow their advice without question, however often it had proven impractical or even destructive.

One of his strangest characteristics was his attitude towards money. He felt that any funds turned over to him as an investment in the firm were to be used in any way he arbitrarily saw fit. To him, the prime purpose of a business was to fulfill certain social purposes. A business enterprise should have several goals. It should provide an adequate income for workers so that they could support their families. Workers were entitled to decent housing, a chance at education, health care and constructive leisure time. That business or agriculture should also make a profit seemed to him entirely secondary. And down-right sinful was the idea that the major share of profits from any enterprise should be used by the owner or the owner's family to live in luxury and ostentation. His austere, restrained upbringing stayed with him his whole life—as long as he were permitted to do exactly as he pleased.

This unorthodox approach to the business world had to be balanced against his exceptional ability as a political thinker. His more conservative colleagues would roll their eyes heavenward when they would listen to him expounding ideas which seemed to them too bizarre or too impractical to consider seriously. He could convince them perhaps that the capitalist system was full of defects: it was based on inequities, subject to boom and bust, rewarded ruthlessness and too often even deception. But to persuade the members of the Chamber of Commerce to begin to pay income taxes was a concept which the ruling class could not bring themselves to do. So the government had to raise its revenues through a tax on almost everything the country imported, however heavily that tax fell on the poor and the unprotected.

Like every chief executive, Figueres had his particular ways of leading. At Cabinet meetings he, or a Minister, would present a problem, economic, political, religious or, in the case of a natural calamity, physical. The Cabinet would discuss the situation. Pepe would go around the room asking each man in turn what he thought should be done. Often the solutions would coincide with his. When a majority agreed on a certain course of action, there would be no problem. But if most of the members wanted something Pepe did not agree with, he used a technique which was unassailable.

He let them talk, argue, bring up objections, make suggestions. He listened carefully—or at least seemed to—fixing the speaker with a kind of hypnotic stare. No objection ever showed on his face; he appeared to be absorbed in what the minister was saying and would seem to concentrate on every syllable. Then he would ask a question.

"Are you really convinced that lowering the wages of the banana workers is the policy we should follow?" Somehow the tone of voice implied doubt, though that was never openly expressed. The man addressed would hesitate a moment, then marshal his forces and try to sound convincing while the blue X ray eyes pinned him to his chair. In spite of everything, his voice would become weaker and weaker, and his arguments less cogent.

Finally Figueres would say, his voice full of regret, "Oh, I'm so sorry but I understood that we had agreed not to lower their wages, so I've already spoken to the press. But don't worry. We'll discuss it some more and see what we can do."

* * * * * * * * * *

For a long time Figueres had visualized a school lunch program which would supply two meals a day to poor children. Since malnutrition was a wide-spread problem in Costa Rica, he believed that only through a government plan could a well balanced diet be guaranteed to those in need. He was fascinated with several studies about the relationship between malnutrition and the inability of children to learn within the school room. Worse still, the permanent effects of prolonged malnutrition on the child's mental development during the early years of life were frightening in their implications for society. He was determined to try to fight the insidious inroads of poverty and hunger which were leaving an underclass with little hope for the future.

As always, the political problems intervened. Congress would have to vote the funds for the program and there was the usual horse trading in which politicos swapped a vote for this in exchange for that. In addition, the problems of organization, management and above all, supply at first seemed overwhelming. But as the weeks passed the problems were slowly solved and every child whose family lived below a certain economic level was provided with two hot meals a day.

The groundwork for another favorite project was laid during the time of the Junta. It was the Family Assistance Program which had a unique twist. To a household below the poverty line, the government support system channeled the money directly into the hands of the mother of the family, rather than to the father. It was assumed that the mother would use the money more wisely in caring for the children and would spend it on food, shoes and medicines rather than on brief encounters at the neighborhood bar.

This was considered by many to be evidence of a great leap forward in a machista society. That Congress would even consider a measure like this, implying that women were more responsible than men in family matters, aroused in some men intense opposition.

"How is it possible that the money will come to the mothers instead of the fathers? That's unnatural. He's the head of the household." Evidence to the contrary, the classic machista arguments were trotted out against the idea, emotions roared and thundered against the concept, and loud objections reverberated through the halls of Congress. Little by little the logic of the program prevailed, but it was several years before lawmakers could be persuaded. Although Pepe was president twice more after that, he did not occupy the presidency when the program was finally implemented. The failure of Congress to vote the project into law during his time in office was a source of bitter disappointment to him.

* * * * * * * *

The final break with Marten came only seven short months into the Junta's administration. As so often happens in what seems a passing disagreement, no one could foresee what would be the painful denouement of this situation from its ordinary beginning. The discussion which finally lead to the end of the friendship began like so many other arguments in a meeting of the Junta, this time in the offices of the Foreign Ministry.

The government was facing yet another economic crisis. As the members of the Junta were discussing what to do, Alberto walked in, holding a sheaf of papers. He was his usual self, elegant and controlled, his lawyer's face carefully impassive. Putting his briefcase on the central table, he pushed aside a small tray with coffee cups and laid the papers face down in front of his chair. The Minister of Education who had been quoting some statistics about the need for more funding for primary and secondary schools, stopped in the middle of a sentence.

Without an apology for the interruption Alberto picked up his papers, looked around at his fellow ministers to be sure that he had their attention, and made an announcement.

"I have here the solution to our economic problems."

"All right," Pepe said, looking interested. "Let's hear them."

"Yes," said Fernando Valverde, Minister of the Interior, "we can discuss them right now."

Marten turned to stare for a moment at Valverde, hardly able to hide his contempt. He was convinced that Valverde's intellectual development was only slightly above that of the anthropoid apes.

"I didn't come here to listen to a discussion. The ideas are all worked out and are complete in every detail. They don't need further comment. They only need the Junta's vote to begin to implement them".

For a moment no one said anything. Then Pepe asked the question they were all framing.

"Are you expecting us to accept your ideas without even knowing what they are?"

Slowly Marten began to gather up his papers and to slide them back into his briefcase.

"I've already told you. There is no need for an explanation or a discussion. Just a vote. That's the only thing that's necessary."

"But vote on what?" demanded Padre Nuñez, his voice getting angry. "We don't even know what you're asking us to vote on!"

Alberto stood up.

"I've heard enough of this! I'm going back to my office."

The door closed behind him.

Later that afternoon Pepe phoned just before yet another set of diplomats were coming to call. "I've invited Alberto to have dinner with us. About seven. Please have Lila keep the children out of the way."

When Marten arrived he was the same as he always was with me; in a kind of formal way he was warm and sweet, full of compliments as befitted the relationship with the wife of his oldest friend.

"You should always wear that shade. The color suits you perfectly."

At dinner we were cautious to avoid any subject which might slip into controversy. With delicate footwork the three of us tiptoed around all matters which might even suggest disagreement; we knew that if we lowered our guard just by a millimeter one of the men might imply something which would shatter the shaky truce. This technique lead to a few prolonged silent passages while we served ourselves to yet another helping of food we really didn't want, and asked each other for the salt which we then didn't use, but at least the dinner survived without any heavy artillery blasting the china off the table.

Just as we were having coffee Daniel Oduber came in.

He was a complex man who looked like Othello but had the soul of Iago. Drivingly ambitious, he was indefatigable in his pursuit of power, and at this stage in his career, was president of Congress. As such he worked closely with Pepe in attempts to coerce or to persuade Congress to go along with the decrees which the Junta was passing. He was witty and clever in both English and Spanish, and had recently returned from McGill University in Montreal with a new wife and a new Master's degree in Philosophy. He worked hard at finding out who was doing what to whom, and though he made fun of everybody, he was determined to become rich and powerful, no matter how twisted the road to the goal.

The three men took their coffee into the study and I left them alone. I knew that Daniel had the latest news and gossip of the Congress which he would vouchsafe with accompanying mockery and derision. But later I got a full account of the final conversation with Marten, first from Pepe and then from Daniel.

Pepe still hoped that some kind of compromise could be worked out, some way found to reestablish the relationship which had formed a fundamental part of his life. He tried to sound conciliatory.

"Why did you demand that the Junta accept your proposals without any discussion? Or even without our knowing what they were."

"I've explained it to you. Nobody in the Junta, with the exception of Padre Nuñez, has studied economics. Why let them waste my time talking about something they don't understand? They're not capable of adding anything to the discussion."

"Even if you think they're not capable of adding anything to the discussion, they must at least be informed about the decrees they're being asked to support— informed before you expect them to give their consent. Think about it a minute. You certainly wouldn't consent if the situation were reversed."

They went over it and over it, each side refusing to see that there was something to be said for another point of view. There seemed no way out of the impasse. Alberto, his rage mounting steadily, lit a cigarette, took two puffs and put it out. The silence settled down as the three tried to decide how to extricate themselves from a situation which was becoming increasingly painful. By now they were all exhausted, partly from the tension of the encounter and partly because they all worked long hours under unremitting pressure. The nature of their work compelled them to solve intractable social problems within as brief a time as possible, with no hours left for R & R.

It was Alberto who finally solved the problem.

"We're not getting anywhere," he said, putting his gold cigarette lighter away. To a large extent he had ignored Oduber and had spent most of the evening addressing himself to Pepe. "What I perceive is that we disagree about everything. And what you really want is for me to resign."

Caught by surprise Pepe stared at him without moving. He was stunned by the suggestion, wondering if it had been made seriously or if this were a twisted kind of joke. Would Alberto add something, clarify, explain his words? But no one said anything. There was something almost menacing in the quiet. The room suddenly felt hot. Oduber told me later that he thought he was choking. The three of them avoided looking at each other as they waited, trying to think of some way to break the spell.

Alberto especially waited. Months later he revealed that he had expected Pepe to protest, to object immediately, or at least to ask him to reconsider. He had hoped that Figueres would suggest that he not act too hastily and to think of the consequences for all of them, especially for the government. What he seemingly wanted was el puente de oro, the golden bridge, which would permit him to retreat gracefully, saving his dignity and his pride.

But Pepe was too shaken to respond. Nothing broke the silence. He sat without moving as they all waited for a miracle, for a deus ex machina to appear and lead them out of the predicament.

Finally, hopeless now, Alberto stood up.

"You'll have my resignation tomorrow."

* * * * * * * *

One of the most astute decisions Figueres made was his refusal to fight with the Catholic Church, however much he was emotionally opposed to that organization. (As a boy he was sent to a school run by German priests who used to disciple the boys by beating them in ways which Pepe considered unnecessarily cruel.) He further felt that the Church exploited its adherents, filling them with guilt so that it could maintain control by psychological manipulations. But his objection to open conflict with the Church was based on the grounds that a political leader had to limit the enemies he could hope to defeat. When some members of the Junta urged an open break with the church, Pepe refused to support the idea.

At a cabinet meeting he expressed his objection which became a guiding principle of the Junta. "We can't afford any more enemies. We're confronting now the U.S. State Department on certain issues, the moneyed class within our own society, some of the labor unions and an antagonistic local press. To take on yet another enemy, the Catholic Church, would be a form of madness. Think how much power they have here! What we should try to do is to use them, or at least to do everything possible to neutralize any opposition which we see developing."

To this end he began to cultivate the hierarchy of the Church. He asked permission to visit the Archbishop with whom he held long talks on several occasions in an effort to win his cooperation in helping to carry out certain social reforms. In his speeches he refrained from attacking the Church and emphasized areas where the government and the Church saw eye to eye. And he went willingly to special Te Deums, masses in honor of certain occasions or events which were important both to the religious community and to the society as a whole. He was convinced that many of these religious services helped to unify the country for they brought together in a safe, unthreatening way the various classes and factions who could join together in the celebration of their faith.

One day, not long after he became president, he had to attend a high mass at the Cathedral, a ceremony which was longer and more complicated than a regular mass. When I asked how many years it had been since he had attended a church service, he gave some off-hand answer because it had been so long ago he couldn't remember. But instead of being irritated at having to go to this one, he smiled.

Uh-oh, I thought, whenever he looks that innocent, I know he's planning to do someone in. Who is it this time?

"Why are you so happy about having to participate in something you don't believe in?"

"Because as long as I'm sitting there in the church I can think about something important, such as whom to appoint to a position on the Board of the Central Bank—and nobody can interrupt me! Nobody. That's why I love these High Masses. They go on for hours."

"But what about all the hopping up and down, the kneeling and bowing and praying? That's an interruption."

"Not really. I remember enough from the masses of my childhood, so I sense what's happening. I run on automatic with no breaks in my chain of thought."

It was at one of these High Masses, a special Te Deum, that he made the most important decision of his whole political career. But it was not implemented until after an unexpected event had occurred. Named for Edgar Cardona, the Minister of Defense, and christened the Cardonazo, it caught everyone by surprise and confirmed Pepe's determination to carry out his decision.

216

Chapter XVI

It was doomed to failure, his counter-revolution. An enterprise of such ineptness was almost impossible to imagine especially if devised by a man as blinded by ambition as poor Cardona. How could anyone in Costa Rica at that time (the end of 1948) believe that he could successfully fight against Figueres and the Junta? Not only did the government control almost all the arms but it enjoyed the unquestioning loyalty of most of the population. Furthermore, there was a widespread and impassioned objection to the prospect of another armed struggle. Costa Ricans had reached the end of their patience with wars and rumors of wars, and now they wanted nothing so much as a return to their accustomed tranquility.

But even if Cardona had been a charismatic leader capable of galvanizing his followers to heroic action, I do not believe the revolt would have succeeded. In politics as in love, timing is everything. And for Cardona, the times were out of joint. But more than that, there was the person himself. Although he was a handsome and courageous man, he was also out of his league with the intricacies of politics. He didn't understand that even if he were to succeed in his conquest of power, he would not know what to do with it once it was in his hands. He had no plan for making or carrying out policy, no program, no vaguest notion even of how to proceed as head of a government. It's frightening to realize how often in human affairs men like Cardona are the ones who seize power. And when they do, their domestic and foreign policy can be summed up in three words: I, me, mine.

About the Cardonazo, the attempted coup, I have some very sharp memories, most of them not associated with the fighting. I remember that Cardona demanded four changes in the government: He opposed the nationalization of the banks. He demanded the elimination of the ten percent tax on capital. He insisted on the resignation of Alberto Marten as Minister of Economics and Commerce. He accused Father Nuñez, the Minister of Labor, of being a communist and tried to extract from the Junta the promise that Nuñez would be fired. When his demands were all refused, he began to plot a take-over of the government.

Whatever his explanations later, my perception was that he felt slighted by the other members of the Junta. To be Minister of Defense was not enough, though he loved his fancy uniforms and his shiny black boots. He wanted to be consulted about other issues as well and seemed incapable of realizing that grabbing up a machine gun and fighting in the mountains required certain qualities, which he had in abundance. But after the smoke had cleared, a completely different set of qualities was required in order to govern successfully. And those he did not have.

Pushed by some of the wealthy landowners, he began to meet secretly with a few hotheads. They convinced each other that moving against the Junta would be a swift and brief endeavor, and that before anyone would be aware of what was happening, the whole operation would be over. And Cardona would be president. I did not believe that they were cruel or wicked men. Rather, something much worse. They were dangerous: they were willing to send their followers to their deaths for an ill defined purpose whose success would have dragged the country into another civil war.

My first inkling of anything amiss came just before noon on one of those days so crystal clear it almost tinkled. My younger sister, then about twenty-four, had come down from Alabama for a lengthy visit after finishing college at Montevallo. Up on a second floor terrace at one side of the house she was sunbathing, wearing a two-piece, brilliant green swim suit which did its best to cover the salient points of the compass. Since the terrace was never used except by the family, it hardly seemed to matter much what anybody out there wore or didn't wear.

218

As I was working in my study, there were steps along the wide hall, and then our wonderful housekeeper, Lila, appeared in the doorway. Full of warmth and tenderness, she was softly rounded and well-upholstered, with tousled dark hair and the whitest smile in all of Latin America. One of my gringo friends used to say that she looked like someone you had run away with to a South Sea Island—ten years later. Pausing for a second on the threshold, she turned towards a person I couldn't see and motioned for silence.

"Lila, is lunch ready?"

"Not quite, Señora. But here are some soldiers who say they were sent to protect the house."

"But we already have our regular guards."

"These are others. There's some kind of problem. Colonel Cardona is—he's trying to—they're calling it a revolution."

"Cardona!" I stopped myself from saying that she must have been mistaken because the colonel was not capable of thinking his way out of a paper bag, much less of organizing a revolution. Instead, I walked to the door. Down the hall there seemed to be wall to wall soldiers, each with a rifle. "Where are they supposed to go?"

The sergeant in charge stepped forward.

"Señora, with your permission, we do our duty." He turned to his faithful followers. "This way."

Before I could stop him, he was moving towards the terrace, the others clumping behind.

By the time I got there, all six soldiers had crowded onto the open porch. Transfixed, frozen with astonishment, they stared down at Annie Laurie, who was lying on a large towel, calmly reading a history of Costa Rica. As I watched their faces I realized that none of the soldiers had ever seen a bikini bathing suit before, and that probably none of them had ever been close to a blond foreign woman, with or without layers of clothing. She looked up and smiled and then said two of her seven Spanish words.

"Buenos días."

They acknowledged her greeting mutely, still incapable of speech. The silence stretched out. I wondered what was going to happen, how the sergeant would ever be able to break the magic spell which had imprisoned his stalwart troops, or if they would be found in that same stupefied position decades later when they had all finally turned to stone. But I needn't have worried. One of the soldiers, at last able to breathe and bent on sacrificing himself, took a step forward.

"Sergeant, I am willing to remain here, dangerous as it is."

Brave enough to confront danger head on, he looked down into the street below. "Sergeant, as you are able to see, from here I could shoot anyone coming towards the house."

Impressed by the courage of his companion, a second soldier spoke up. "I also could remain here."

"Me, too," said Number three, and in the flutter of a coffee leaf, all six had volunteered for the hardship post.

"Just a minute," the sergeant snapped. What he was about to add was lost in a rattle of gunfire coming from across town. We listened, trying to decide how far away the shooting was. That is, Lila and I listened, while the platoon remained in its zombie-like state. In which direction would the shooting move? And who was it? None of the young soldiers exhibited the slightest interest in our possible imminent demise; they were still mesmerized. Annie Laurie didn't even speak walking-around Spanish, so she had no inkling of what was happening, and simply accepted soldiers and distant gunfire as part of the scenery.

After a moment I realized that the only way to get those men off that terrace and to their defensive posts around the house would be for her to leave. So I suggested that she take up her towel and beat a retreat down the hall to her room. She stood up and started towards the door, every head pulled in her direction like iron filings following a magnet. But once the door was closed behind her, military discipline slipped back into place and the sergeant was able to move his erstwhile puppets at least out of the house and into the garden.

One of the comforting things about the domesticity of our lives at that time was that it rolled relentlessly along, undeflected by wars, revolutions, crises or distant gunfire. The children raced in, chattering and insistent, begging to have lunch with me and Aunt Lolly since Papá wasn't going to be at home. Then Lila reappeared to say that lunch was served. If Pepe were at home, he didn't like having three-and-five year old children around who spilled food on the tablecloth and who sometimes talked when he wanted to be talking; so usually they ate in the servants' dining room. But on the occasions when he was away, they took advantage of his absence and were allowed to sit at the table and play grown-up.

"Where's Pepe?" Annie Laurie asked.

"He left early this morning for the Presidential House. Aside from the usual dozens of rumors, I don't think he had any idea that anything was happening."

As though to emphasize how unexpected life was, the sound of gunfire increased. It didn't seem to be any closer, although it was hard to tell exactly where it was coming from. There was just more of it, mixed now with the sound of guns heavier than semi-automatic rifles. I began to make vague plans about leaving town with the kids, which car to take with which driver, which roads to follow that would probably not yet be blocked off. Needless to say, we would go as fast as we could towards La Lucha.

Lunch was just ending when there was a phone call for me.

"Pepe, what's happening? Where are you? Are you all right?"

"That goddam Cardona! I should have known better than to trust him!"

"But where are you?"

"I can't tell you over the phone, but I'll send word later. That damn fool has closed himself up in the Penitencería (a fort and prison complex on the road to the airport). Some of the other crazies are with him. It's the worst mistake he could have made. All we have to do now is wait. We'll shut off the water, food, electricity, everything. It's just a matter of hours....Poor idiot! I already feel sorry for him."

Pepe was right. It was just a matter of hours, less than twenty-four. Some time before dawn the next day, Cardona must have realized it was all over. When the water and light were cut off, and he received word that Pepe was planning to start shelling the fort if he didn't surrender, he knew there was no further hope. Whether he had expected a general uprising throughout the country, or if he had thought that Costa Ricans would accept an armed revolt against the Junta and calmly go on about their business, I never found out. Perhaps he himself had not even thought it necessary to plan that far ahead.

A white flag was raised over the fort and the gates were opened. Pepe drove in at the wheel of his favorite form of transportation, an open Jeep. The surrender was short and swift. Poor Cardona. Instead of his usual performance of the gay blade about town, he was silent now, almost immobile, head hunched down, incapable of facing anyone. My memory of him during the Revolution was that even in the weeks of fighting when everyone else was covered with grime, he had always managed to have a spotless uniform. Now he was dirty. And wrinkled. With a dark growth of beard and, on the elegantly trimmed moustache, dust and bits of paper.

After the Cardonazo, Pepe was often asked why he had picked a man like Cardona as Minister of Defense. People tended to forget that he had fought bravely during the Revolution and that he had a group of blind followers who looked to him for leadership. (Or maybe just as a drinking buddy.) And within that group, he had considerable influence. But after this, whenever his name came up and Pepe's choice of him as a Cabinet member was questioned, he had a stock answer.

"I know So-and-So is not a genius. And I would much prefer to have Jesus Christ or at least Abraham Lincoln as one of my Ministers. But since neither of them has come forward, I'm going to stick with the ones I have."

And from that day forward he always added a post script.

"Except Cardona."

Chapter XVII

In the center of San José is a small fort called the Bella Vista. It is like a slightly shopworn, fairy tale castle, its crenellated walls needing repairs and a round tower at each of the four corners all wanting paint. Faded flags droop in the breeze above the sharply pointed roofs. In the middle of the fort is a flat, open space where squads of soldiers used to drill. Here, in December of 1948, took place the most important event of Pepe's three terms as president.

The weather was worthy of the occasion. A sparkling, newly minted day glittered around the fort as the invited guests took their places in the rows of chairs set out in the open mid section. Against one crenellated wall a small platform, like a stage, had been erected so the speakers could be seen and heard by all the dignitaries. The members of the cabinet were there, the judges of the Supreme Court, the members of Congress, the Papal Nuncio and the senior churchmen, the entire diplomatic corps, the business and professional leaders of the country, several large contingents of official representatives from Central and South America,—and enough news media people to prevent the loss of a single deathless word. (Some of them may have wondered why there was a heavy sledgehammer leaning against Pepe's chair.) Over to one side a small drum-and-bugle corps stood more or less at attention, whispering among themselves.

I took my seat in the section reserved for the Cabinet members and their wives. Through a chain of events which I cannot now clearly recall, I had a buyer in New Orleans who bought clothes for me. She had infallible taste, unrelentingly elegant, and whenever I wore something she had purchased, I felt that I was the envy of all. On this occasion I remember wearing her latest offering, a beige linen dress with a small white collar and cuffs, one of those simple, flowing things for which you know you've paid too much and are glad you did.

Pepe occupied the middle chair on the platform. As I came in he smiled a greeting, a somewhat startling departure from his normal behavior. When we were in public together, he usually displayed toward me all the warmth and spontaneity of the head undertaker dealing with a wayward subordinate. To his right sat the Minister of Education, to his left, the Minister of the Army holding a rolled up document looking like a scroll. At a signal from Pepe, the bugle corps let out a somewhat quavering bleat on their instruments followed almost at once by the percussion section which drummed out a mighty roll. Heads snapped around, whispering stopped in mid sentence and papers rattled themselves into pocket and purse.

Stepping rapidly to a small microphone at the edge of the platform, Pepe made a few welcoming remarks and then motioned to the ministers on either side of him to come forward. The Minister of War wore his army uniform, the Minister of Education, a former high school teacher, was dressed in a dark blue, pin striped suit. Pepe's words rang out across the upturned faces.

"Today, the government of Costa Rica officially disbands all of its armed forces. From now on we will have no air force, no army and no navy. Too often in Latin America, armies have been used by dictatorial regimes to crush opposition and to intimidate their own people. The governing Junta in Costa Rica has no reason to fear its citizens and therefore feels that guns are not required in order to remain in power."

Then he made one of his unexpected and dramatic gestures. Walking to the back of the stage, he took up the sledgehammer which had leaned against his chair and swung it as hard as he could against a section of the wall just above the platform. There was a grinding of stone on stone, a moment of suspense as the section leaned outward, and then a collective sigh accompanied the teetering rocks as one by one they toppled downward and crashed into an open field below the high wall. Only a few of us knew that he had sent a crew of men the day before to loosen the stones so that they would be sure to fall and not ruin his theatrical performance.

He returned to the front of the platform. Turning to the Minister of War, he held out his hand and received the scroll-like document the official had been holding.

"This paper officially transfers the Bella Vista Fortress to the Ministry of Education. The Junta has already started appropriating money for the Ministry so that it can transform this fort into what we hope will become the most beautiful museum in Latin America."

He handed the document to the Education Minister who unrolled it and held it up for the audience to see. There was an impressive collection of enough official stamps, red seals, small flags and illegible Nineteenth Century script to make the transfer seem binding enough to withstand any legislative attempts to rescind or to disavow it.

Then the Minister stepped forward. Rare among his colleagues, Uladislao Gamez was blond, fair skinned and blue eyed, revealing his descent from Polish and Spanish ancestors who came from their country's northern provinces. He delivered a graceful little speech saying that today's ceremony was the culmination of an age-old dream, that throughout the centuries humanity had pursued the ideal of a world without war and that with the disbanding of its armed forces, Costa Rica had taken the first step towards realizing that goal. His final sentence later acquired an ironic twist we could not have foreseen, given the state of the arms race in the world today.

"We hope Costa Rica will serve as an example for other countries around the globe and that we will see one unarmed nation after another decide to follow our same golden road to peace and prosperity."

To my surprise, the applause was not wildly enthusiastic. I turned to Francisco Orlich, the Minister of Public Works, and whispered, "Why aren't they clapping?"

Orlich may have had his defects but being verbose was not one of them. He usually parceled words out with an eyedropper.

"Most of these guys come from military dictatorships. It's their armies that keep them in power. They think Pepe's crazy to do this."

I glanced over at the foreign visitors and watched the sun glinting off the brass buttons on all the uniforms. They looked well fed and well dressed as they stood close together, more than a little bewildered by a country which was suggesting that they all be put out of business and be forced to spend their time actually working at something constructive. From the unsmiling faces I gathered that the concept of disarmament left them singularly unenthusiastic.

On the other hand, the American diplomats, coming from a country with the largest military force in the world, were caught in a dilemma: they were staunch allies of Costa Rica and felt that they had to support the only true democracy in Latin America. But disband all your armed forces and try to persuade others to do the same? ... As for the Costa Ricans, most of them were taken by surprise, for complete disarmament at that time was a startling idea and though they were traditionally not militaristic, still—no army at all? My memory is that the warmest applause came from the members of the Cabinet and from the representatives of the Church, with the rest of the audience either abstaining altogether, or else being reluctantly polite.

Forty years later, that gesture has proven to be the single most important achievement of the Figueres presidencies. Instead of wasting their resources on insane acquisitions of firepower and military materiel, the society has invested its taxes in socially beneficial programs. There are schools everywhere throughout the country and Costa Rica has a higher literacy rate than the United States. An electric grid covers the nation from border to border so that electricity is available in even the most remote regions. A network of roads links all parts of the country. The rural health care system is used as a model for many Third World countries. This health system is coordinated with programs for school lunches, family planning and support for the handicapped and the indigent.

In the cultural field there are ballet companies, small theaters, and a Youth Orchestra all supported by the national government. Any child who demonstrates musical talent will be trained at government expense and then incorporated into the Youth Orchestra. Once a year the orchestra makes a tour outside of Costa Rica, sometimes to Mexico, or to South America, or to the United States, and all of the players' expenses are paid for out of public taxes.

And finally, there is a system of National Parks. One eighth of the country's total area has been turned over to the park system which protects the unique and priceless array of birds, plants, orchids, green turtles, rain forests and, in one case, black sand beaches which are found nowhere else on earth. Environmentalists from all over the world come to study the country's natural riches and to admire a system of preservation which is constantly developing techniques for better care of Nature's treasures.

I do not suggest that these programs would not have been carried out if the Army had been kept in place. I do suggest that progress would have been much slower. For example, no other country in Central America has an electric grid covering the whole country, or a rural health service which can compare with Costa Rica's. And no country south of the Rio Grande has a system of roads providing access to the remotest regions.

By a lovely poetic twist, knocking down the wall of the Bella Vista Fort formed the foundation for the new Costa Rica.

* * * * * * * * *

Last Chapter

Who can explain why a marriage fails? When does communication stop or become reduced to the point of hopelessness? When does the realization come that nothing is working, that one or both partners are beginning to feel smothered?

I had known for years that Figueres was a political animal. He had demonstrated his obsession over and over; his mind set was locked in that direction. But it was only after repeated shocks that I finally accepted the fact that he was so closely tied to the pursuit of power that little else in life had any value for him.

Furthermore, I came to realize that it was a mistake to think that extraordinary men would respond towards marriage the way ordinary men did. Just as Scott Fitzgerald wrote that the rich were different from the rest of us, so I became convinced that those infected by the virus of political power were also different. Their values were different. Their goals were different. They viewed the world through lenses which only permitted them to see what would enhance their political ends. Pepe's uniqueness came from his extraordinarily deep commitment to bringing about social change and to creating the new Costa Rica he had envisioned for so long. I was aware that it was this quality of statesmanship which distinguished him from the garden-variety politicians who surrounded him. And that he really was different.

I realized that the consuming demands which he, as a leader, was subject to in those days would not allow us to build a family in the seclusion and privacy for which I yearned. I had been caught up in the whirlwind of momentous, historic events, a whirlwind mainly of his creating. And I had slowly come to realize that I would have to choose between living in the whirlwind for many more years, or else settling for a normal family life, even if alone with my children.

All of this had been going through my head for a long time. But I was afraid to take the step. I had lived my whole adult life in Costa Rica, with the exception of the two years Pepe and I had spent in exile, and the idea of going it alone with two small children terrified me. Martí and Muni were nine and seven. What would a break do to them? Where were we going to live? How?

The weeks slipped away. Pepe was busy organizing and reorganizing a new political party, el Partido de Liberación Nacional. It was the first time in the history of Central America that a political party in the American or European sense of the word was coming into being. Until then there had only been temporary groupings around a presidential candidate which would dissolve as soon as the elections were over. During the campaign the party would be called after the candidate's name, the Calderonistas or the Picadistas, but until Figueres, no one had ever tried to set up a political party which would exist between elections and which would have a permanent form.

It was a difficult matter to bring to fruition. First, convincing people that a permanent party would have political advantages was confusing because the concept was so new. After the campaign the Caudillo, the leader, would reward those who had helped him win the election with the fruits of victory, public office, government contracts, the appointment to an embassy abroad, or access to the levers of power at home. To a small society in which political life had always been an intensely personal matter and founded on personal loyalty, the idea of a permanent party seemed too cold to be acceptable. It was forbiddingly foreign. Secondly, the notion that even between campaigns a party would require time and money to continue functioning seemed to bewilder Pepe's supporters, however committed they were. Why should they continue to contribute? What did he need money for? What would party volunteers or employees do for two or three years between elections? Why did one need an organization just sitting there when no campaigning was going on?

It was exactly the kind of situation which attracted him. The challenge was enormous; the chances of success were relatively small because the arms he had to fight with were not very powerful and his allies were few. Of course, he had the examples of the European political parties and those of the U. S. and of England. But to his followers, Europe and the U. S. all seemed far away. As had so often happened he had envisioned change and as before, he had mainly himself to rely on.

An endless round of meetings began. I confessed to a feeling of déjà vu, for it was the same process as had gone on in raising money for the purchase of arms, for planning the revolution, for organizing the Junta government. It became his one topic of conversation, his only interest, his obsession. Just as the wonders of the fireplace during the early months of our marriage had enthralled him, so now anyone who came to discuss any other matter was subjected to a barrage of arguments about the need for a permanent political party. That the other person might have no interest in politics and had rather come to talk about a financial or even a personal matter was of no moment. The need for a permanent political party was the only acceptable topic of conversation. And once again it was this same relentless, driving dedication which would prove to be his key to success.

* * * * * * * *

For some time I had been having a physical problem which had begun not long after Muni's birth. My mother had suffered over a period of years from a form of cancer which seemed to have gone into remission but which was always there, something malevolent and frightening, ready to strike when least expected.

I found myself becoming increasingly fearful that the same thing would develop in me.

When I went for an examination the doctor's verdict was not reassuring. "There's something there but I can't tell what yet. We'll just have to watch and wait until there are more symptoms."

"But let's do something! Please. We could begin treatment right away and maybe head it off."

But he could not be moved. He was cool and calm, his air of control like a thick blanket covering the whole office and smothering any suggestions he had not thought of himself. I suspected he didn't know what to do, but since he was the best cancer specialist in the country, his opinion carried enough conviction to keep me silent. Besides, would another specialist in another consultation be able to do or say anything more reassuring if there were not enough evidence yet to find something to treat?

I went home. We were living at the time in a big house on a street which lead out to San Pedro, one of the small towns surrounding the capital. As always when facing a crisis, I asked the maid for coffee. Sitting in the upstairs living room I looked out over the rooftops of the city towards the western mountains darkening against the flames of a sunset sky. This time of the evening always made me sad as a special loneliness seemed to take possession of the house. The children had gone somewhere with Lila, the housekeeper, and the sounds of the traffic drifting in from below were muted after the rush hour.

I wondered where Pepe was. Perhaps at a meeting somewhere talking about the need for a permanent political party. He had never kept regular hours during his working life so his comings and goings were always subject to impulsive changes. The maids had been trained to have food ready at any hour of the day or night. Since he never cared what he ate he was satisfied with black beans and rice so long as it was hot and could be prepared quickly. I decided to wait for him to have my dinner, planning to put the kids to bed after they had eaten their supper.

There was a phone call at that moment from Lila. "Señora, los chiquitos quieren pasar la noche con mi familia." Once or twice a month they went to her house to spend the night and enjoyed every minute of it.

"Y la escuela?" I asked, enquiring about school.

"Estamos en la casa temprano mañana." Her ready response about bringing the kids back early the next morning hardly gave me the time to go through the motions of consent.

I settled down with a book for a long wait, but to my surprise the wait was short. There was the sound of the car coming, doors opening and closing, and then Pepe's hurried footsteps on the stairs. He began to talk as he came into the room.

"I had a very positive meeting, very encouraging. They seem to be slowly getting the idea. Could you ask someone to bring some dinner. up here. I haven't eaten since early this morning."

I told the maid to bring some food upstairs, and then turned to him. "I spoke to the doctor today."

"Oh." He picked up the phone and started dialing. After a moment he said into the mouthpiece, "Chico, come over, can you? I need to discuss something."

The maid appeared with a tray and put it on a table near him. Still talking on the phone he began to eat, swiftly, absently, not being aware of anything about the food, just satisfied that it hadn't taken too long to prepare. "We can also go over a few figures. I may have to borrow some more money from you."

Chico evidently used some of his favorite vulgar expressions because Pepe laughed. "I know I owe you—how many millions?—but you're in so deep you can't afford to get out now. Stop screwing around and come on over. And tell Fernando to come too. I'll get in touch with Padre Nuñez."

He hung up. "I have to get some papers for this meeting."

Halfway out the door he stopped. "What did you say about the doctor? What doctor?"

I watched his back disappearing down the hall.

More weeks passed. I went back to the surgeon, had some tests, waited some more for the results, and then received a phone call.

"Señora, the doctor would like to see you tomorrow. Would three o'clock suit you?"

I went into an emotional tailspin. I have cancer! I knew it! Some awful kind they won't even tell me about. I'm going to die! I wanted desperately to talk to someone, almost anyone, to unburden my heart and to seek reassurance. What about my children? Who would take care of them? Brought up by one of Pepe's sisters, the obvious choice, they would forget English, lose touch with their North American heritage, see my family only infrequently, if at all.

But whom could I talk to?

Pepe had gone back to the northern part of the country up near the Nicaraguan border. Having convinced enough people in the central plateau around San José of the need for a new political party, he was making a foray into the distant province of Guanacaste. There were few phones up there; in most cases there was no way to communicate with the cattle farms where he was travelling. Besides, even if there had been ways to get in touch, I didn't know where he was. He was pursuing his usual routine of simply disappearing with no explanation and no estimate of when he would return.

I tried to stop shaking, tried to be rational. Even if I could get in touch with him, what was there to say? Nothing definite yet. Better to wait until after the visit to the doctor the next day to learn what the verdict was.

Being compulsively punctual I arrived early at the physician's office. I walked in to a faint smell of ether mixed with some kind of cleanser. On the wall across the room was a feverish calendar showing the world's cleanest coffee pickers as they gathered beans and exuded a happiness achievable only in paradise. A plastic table held some magazines so tired from patients' hands they lay lifeless and tattered, their smudged pages sticking together for support.

The nurse rustled in, her uniform tight and starched enough to have cracked across her front when she sat down.

"So early!" she said, the accusation in her voice unnerving me still more. She was shapely and dark, and I wondered, without interest, how the medicine man could take his lust away from her long enough to examine any of his patients. Or even if he did. Maybe he just glanced their way and through some other process decided whether or not they needed to be treated. "Siéntese, Señora," she invited me to sit down. "El doctor la ve en un momentico."

I sat down. Under other circumstances I would have tried to figure out whether or not they were sleeping together. I flattered myself that I could usually tell because people's body language frequently betrayed them. Just the way he lit her cigarette, or was too careful not to look at her, or flirted openly with someone else to throw people off—all of that only made it more obvious. But now I didn't care. My only wish was to hear the doctor tell me not to worry because nothing was the matter.

He didn't say that. After a wait which seemed longer than the Pleistocene Age he opened the door to his inner office and silently beckoned me in. With his tanned cheeks and pale curls he looked like a sunburned cherub but turned out to be as unyielding and indifferent as a slave trader. He picked up a large envelope on his desk, twirled it this way and that still without speaking, and then extracted several X rays. Turning his back on me he held one up to the penetrating light coming in a window, picked up another, looked at a third.

"Can you be at the hospital tomorrow morning at five?"

"What? What are you talking about? What's the matter?"

"You told me your mother had uterine cancer. We want to avoid that."

I waited, expecting him to explain further. The silence stretched out. He kept looking at the X rays, absorbed in the black and transparent shapes which were incomprehensible to a lay person, especially one whose mind had gone blank. I waited for him to interpret what he had found which had lead to his decision about operating. I could feel the beginning of the small jerks in my stomach which always shook me whenever I got frightened or worried. Sometimes the shaking brought on hiccoughs or a coughing fit, and then a sniffy nose. Mercifully now nothing happened.

Why didn't he say something instead of just letting me sit there consumed by anxiety? I don't know how long our noiseless interview might have gone on if I hadn't gotten up my courage to ask what his plans for me were.

"What kind of operation are we talking about?"

For a second he looked at me as though I had suggested something indecent. It made me realize that he was used to giving commands, not explanations. Whatever the decision, his patients were supposed to accept it and follow his orders without question. That it was my body which he was going to invade seemingly did not weigh in his thoughts; from the first moments of the earliest examination he had made it clear that the physician alone, in his infinite wisdom, determined what procedure to follow. I wondered if anyone had ever dared to question his judgment, ever suggested that perhaps there was a better way than the one he had selected. It seemed a remote possibility.

"We're talking about the kind of operation your mother should have had several years before she did. This is a hysterectomy. After this, you wont be able to have any more children. Don't eat anything after five o'clock. And be on time tomorrow morning at the hospital. I'm first on the list for the operating room."

I went home. The only person I could think of to call was Pepe's sister, Luisita. Her first words were, "Where's Pepe?"

"He's off somewhere in Guanacaste. I don't know where."

"I'll go with you to the hospital," Luisita said at once. "Come about four-thirty to pick me up. And I'll see that Lila takes good care of the kids. She can bring your gowns and robes from the hospital home to be washed. Don't worry about anything."

At that time the operation lasted about four hours. Patients were kept prone for long periods afterwards because doctors feared that standing upright exerted too much pressure on the incision and the wound would reopen. That meant days and days of inaction, boredom, pain and loneliness. Many visitors came, of course, but that only seemed to retard my recovery: Southerners always have to exude charm from every pore, even in a hospital bed, so being the ingratiating hostess was such a strain it sent my temperature up and up.

In addition, I was consumed with anxiety about my children. Martí especially was attached to me and to be separated for so many days did neither of us any good. I sensed that his visits only increased the pain of our being away from each other. Each time he would stand immobile in the doorway for a few moments while Lila took Muni for a walk down the hall. Then, instead of coming directly to the bed, he took the long way around slowly circling the outer perimeter of the room, all the time keeping his eyes fixed on my face. Finally, at the bedside, he stopped, his hands twisted behind his back.

"Does it hurt?" he asked, his eyes travelling down the white hospital spread.

"Not now."

"Why do you look like that?"

"It's almost all right."

"When are you coming home?"

"In just a few days."

"When?" He reached out one small tanned hand and carefully took hold of mine.

"Come up here."

Watching every move, he climbed up on the high bed. He turned the spread back, his arms slid around me and he nestled down, a long sigh escaping as he seemed to let go. Fear and loneliness flowed away and for a little while he was safe as I rubbed his back, feeling his small, compact body getting heavier as he gradually relaxed. During all the days I was in the hospital the pattern of his visits was always the same, the same circling of the room, the same questions about when I was coming home.

On the second day after the operation Pepe appeared. He was restless and irritable, and I realized that he resented having to make the visit. I wondered how long he would be there. It turned out to be less than ten minutes.

"How do you feel?" he asked, but didn't wait for my answer. Instead, he settled down in a chair, took a newspaper out of his pocket and began to read. After scanning the headlines, he looked up.

"Oh, I've invited some of the boys to meet me here. Chico and Padre Nuñez and—" He stopped as the door opened and the two men he had just mentioned appeared. I knew that they were collaborating in setting up the National Liberation Party.

"Come in, come in," Pepe said, waving them forward. Both approached the bed, held out a hand and asked how I felt. "She's almost well, ready to go home soon."

He pulled two chairs toward the one where he'd been reading. "Sit down. What are those men from Puriscal saying about the money? Will they give any?"

They began to discuss plans for the next few months. They talked about how much money each section of the country would likely contribute, whom they could call on, what groups and organizations could be persuaded to participate, whether or not some of the labor unions might have any interest. Chico agreed to arrange meetings with the coffee growers in his area. After a few minutes Pepe stood up.

"Let's go out into the hall. I want to tell you what happened in Guanacaste."

They went out and I could hear part of a funny story about some of their friends getting drunk in a cantina and trying to pick up a local lady. The laughter had hardly died away when Pepe opened the door to say good-by.

"Well, since there's nothing I can do here, I'm going with Chico to see one or two of his people. I might persuade some of them to contribute something."

The door clicked shut. I listened to the clack of their rapid footsteps receding down the hall and perhaps at that moment I decided to leave. My memory is blurred about the timing because the decision may have been taken the year before and it had simply required all those intervening months to harden enough to bear the weight of my determination. I cannot be sure except that the resolution to leave became firmer and firmer as the hours passed. I lay there in my hospital bed and knew that my days in Costa Rica were numbered. And the knowledge broke my heart.

Since my early twenties I had lived in Costa Rica and almost the only friends I had were there. Moving somewhere else meant ripping my life apart, leaving most of the people who were dear to me, and in a sense starting over. It meant looking for new friends, weaving together the strands of trust and mutual interest, discovering excitement and stimulation for the mind, and most of all, trying to find solace for inescapable loneliness and nourishment for the hungry heart.

On another level it meant finding solutions to all kinds of practical problems. Where was a house, a school, a place to work, a whole network of contacts? I reflected that aside from the shattering emotional impact, the painful thing about moving was that all one's life-support systems were destroyed. How long would it take to find the right doctor or dentist? Or the little lady around the corner to take up a skirt? Or the place that sold that wonderful, home-made bread? They would all be left behind while the person moving had to continue bereft and unprotected into a strange, new place.

Most painful of all, how could I tell my children that we were leaving? Their lives were going to be torn apart because their friends and family would be taken from them. No more weekends in La Lucha. Horseback riding and soccer games and birthday parties up on the third floor (with or without the brown and white goat) and trips to the beach would all disappear. I became aware we were going to live on a small income, without a car, without servants, without a country house. And what we would miss most of all, the web of warmth and tenderness which a Latin family weaves about its members.

Several more months passed. Though I had to wait many weeks before I recovered from the operation, I had to wait even longer to reach the point of certainty about leaving.

I still faced the most difficult task of all, telling Pepe of my decision. Before mentioning it, however, I went out to La Lucha to box up a few things, mainly books and clothes. Out there I realized that I was leaving our marriage with what I had brought to it, except in one all-important aspect: I now had two children who were going with me.

Back in town I began to pack. As I was driven around the city on my last errands before leaving, everything seemed to be subtly different. I couldn't explain how or why but I felt as though I were seeing my surroundings for the first time, and no spot could have been more beautiful. I knew that most of San José was ugly, the streets narrow and uninteresting, the parks needing attention and too many public buildings either undistinguished or else requiring maintenance and paint. But it seemed to my tear-filled eyes that I was looking at a place of indescribable elegance and grace which I would long for endlessly over the passing years.

My airline reservations had been made back to Birmingham and now there were only a few days left. Still I didn't have the courage to tell Muni and Martí that we were leaving permanently. I couldn't bear to hurt them with a blow this devastating so I let them think that this was to be just a short trip like the others we had made. Somehow I pictured that later on it would be easier for them to accept my decision and so would suffer less after they had had time to adjust to all the new circumstances in their lives. Though it was the coward's way, and in the end probably hurt them more, I didn't have the strength at that time to do anything else.

The final days with Pepe were one endless stretch of agony. We were lost in a pathless wilderness in which we couldn't talk to each other, couldn't express any feeling at all, not pain or regret or even anger. We simply regarded each other across an unbridgeable gulf, each encased in a block of ice which froze our hearts and made the simplest effort at communicating an unbearable effort. Carefully, softly we tiptoed around each other, not daring to bring up anything which would tear apart the fragile surface of our daily lives. I felt as though I were drowning in a black morass from which there was no way to escape. Since I knew he would not change his lifestyle even in minor ways, I could think of nothing else to do except to leave and so end my suffering—and his.

He did not ask me to stay. He did not once say that he regretted our failure to create a satisfactory marriage or that he would try to help me make our lives together have more emotional comfort and delight. The night before I left there still seemed nothing to say. We got ready for bed as the deafening silence closed down around us and the familiar feeling of helplessness made my blood congeal. Through the half open door of the closet I could see my clothes for the next day hanging together on the otherwise empty rod which in its nakedness seemed a hundred yards long.

Our suitcases were packed and our tickets and passports stamped and ready. As I checked them once more Pepe sat down on the edge of the bed and without looking at me made only one comment. I had the feeling that we hadn't looked at each other in months, or paid much attention to what the other was saying. Now his voice was distant and remote.

"You have dealt me a blow from which I will never recover," he said. "This is a wound which will never heal."

Suddenly, without warning, he was crying, the tears sliding down his cheeks with no attempt at concealment or subterfuge. He didn't try to brush them away, didn't sob or make any sound; he just sat there immobile while the front of his pale blue shirt showed dark spots from the falling tears.

I had never seen him cry before, not during our exile nor the struggles of the revolution; not even when he was being accused of every crime in the universe by his political enemies. In the face of mounting calamities he had preserved a sphinx-like control, only permitting himself anger or sadness when it was useful in achieving a political goal. Now, too surprised to move, I could only watch him silently, while the chill quietness in the room seemed to sink closer and closer to zero.

Our ride to the airport the next morning was nearly wordless. Martí and Muni sat on either side of him with the chauffeur and the guard in the front seat. Since the children had been trained not to talk when he was in the car, neither of them spoke. I watched the brilliant shrubs and flowers roll by, the Flame of the Forest in spectacular bloom, the scent of orange blossoms faint and delicate receding and returning from gardens along our way. A spotless sky overhead, blue as only a tropical sky can be, was indifferent and remote, untouched by any paltry tragedy on earth, its very perfection proclaiming our unimportance in the universe. Why couldn't there have been an earthquake or at least a raging storm to herald my departure? But a more beautiful day had never been provided.

The memories of my final moments are now blurred, probably because they are too painful to recall. I remember only a boundless number of hands to shake and cheeks to kiss before boarding the aircraft, everyone convinced that I would be returning at the end of a month or two because we had hardly told anyone of my decision. Then the endless walk to the flight of steps leading up to the door of the airplane. Climbing the stairs I looked over the guard rail and observed the baggage being loaded, in those days by hand, and saw my grey suitcases with the red stripe being slowly lifted aboard. I remembered my delight on receiving them as a present for that birthday in college, and now they were accompanying me once again as we set out on another journey.

The end

In commemoration of 100 years of José "Don Pepe" Figueres

Henrietta Boggs 1948

Henrietta Boggs and her children,
Muni and José Martí

José Martí and Muni

Henrietta Boggs and kids

Muni And José Martí

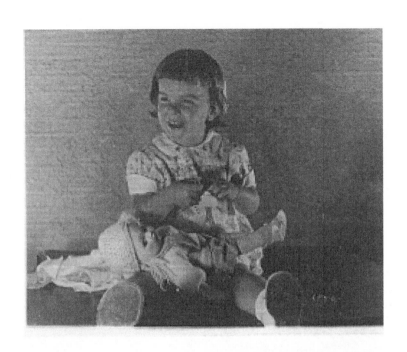

Muni

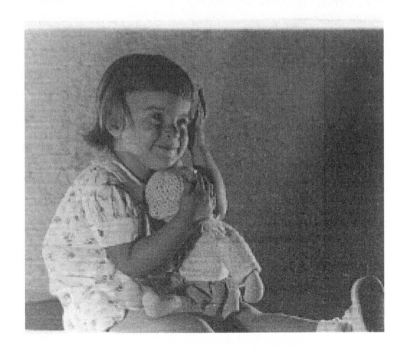

José Martí
and Muni

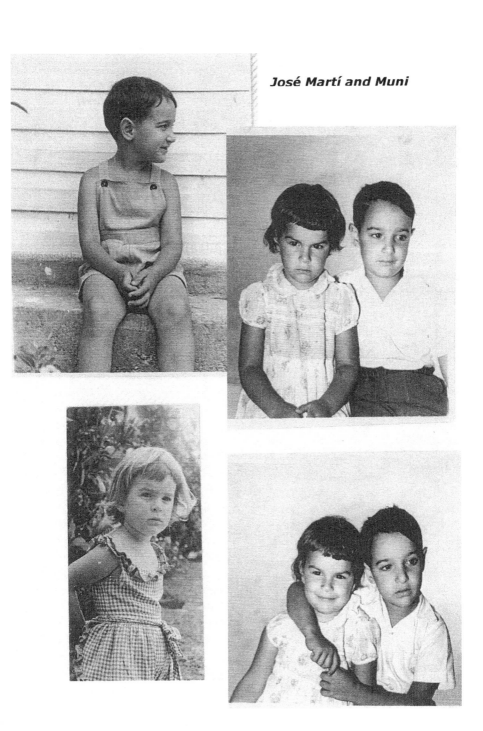

José Martí and Muni

251

**Muni And
José Martí**

Don Pepe, Henrietta, the kids at La Lucha

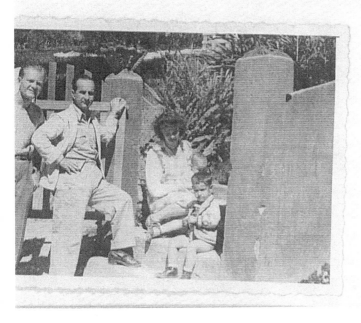

Henrietta Boggs

Henrietta Boggs

José Figueres
Ferrer
1948

Victory Parade, 1948

José Figueres Ferrer, The Symbolic Act Of Abolishing The Armed Forces Of Costa Rica. December 1st 1948

José "Don Pepe" Figueres Ferrer

José "Don Pepe" Figueres Ferrer

*José "Don Pepe" Figueres Ferrer,
Presidential Inauguration*

José "Don Pepe" Figueres Ferrer,
Presidential Dinner

La Lucha Sin Fin, 1936

263

José "Don Pepe" Figueres Ferrer
Regarded As
Father Of The Second Republic Of Costa Rica.

Henrietta Boggs
1st, First Lady
Of The Second Republic Of Costa Rica.